Betty Crocker

simply
salad

100 Healthy and Delicious Recipes

WILEY

Wiley Publishing, Inc.

Library of Congress Cataloging-in-Publication Data
Betty Crocker simply salad : 100 healthy and delicious recipes.
    p. cm.
  Includes index.
  ISBN 978-1-4351-2570-4 (cloth)
  1. Salads. I. Crocker, Betty.
  TX740.B518 2010
  641.8'3—dc22
                                            2010013138

General Mills

Editorial Director:
Jeff Nowak

Publishing Manager:
Christine Gray

Editor:
Grace Wells

Recipe Development and Testing:
Betty Crocker Kitchens

Photography: General Mills Photography Studios and Image Library

Wiley Publishing, Inc.

Publisher: Natalie Chapman

Associate Publisher: Jessica Goodman

Executive Editor: Anne Ficklen

Editor: Meaghan McDonnell

Production Manager: Mike Olivo

Production Editor: Abby Saul

Cover Design: Suzanne Sunwoo

Art Director: Tai Blanche

Layout: Indianapolis Composition Services

Manufacturing Manager: Tom Hyland

Printed in China
10 9 8 7 6 5 4 3 2 1

Our Betty Crocker Kitchens seal guarantees success in your kitchen. Every recipe has been tested in America's Most Trusted Kitchens™ to meet our high standards of reliability, easy preparation and great taste.

Cover photo: Gingered Chicken and Fruit Salad (page 86)

Find more great ideas at *BettyCrocker*.com

Dear Friends,

For many, a meal seems incomplete without a crisp, fresh salad to accompany it! Whether you are looking for a great first course, side dish or main dish salad, you're guaranteed to find a recipe to suit your tastes.

Is there anything more refreshing than a crisp, fresh fruit or vegetable salad, especially on a hot summer day? At your next outdoor party or picnic, treat family and friends to Cold Cucumber Salad or Key West Fruit Salad! When your favorite fruits and vegetables are out of season, try healthy, hearty vegetarian salads like Warm Tuscan Bean Salad and Tabbouleh.

While Caesar Salad and Italian Pasta Salad are classic salads sure to please, Hearty Soybean and Cheddar Pasta Salad and Lo Mein Noodle Salad may become new favorites. Salads like Grilled Steak Potato Salad and Apple Fennel Lobster Salad offer the perfect combination as main dishes—quick and healthy. And don't forget the dressing! For even fresher salad, preparing your own salad dressing is a great—and more economical—option.

With this collection of versatile recipes, every salad you serve will be simply delicious!

Warmly,

Betty Crocker

contents

Salad Basics

Salads have become a mealtime standard. Toss up a starting course of some mixed greens, and mix up a side dish of creamy potato salad or a hearty pasta salad for center stage. But first, brush up on your salad IQ with this helpful information.

Selecting, Storing and Handling Salad Greens

See "Salad Greens Glossary" (page 8) for more information.

- Choose fresh, crisp greens with no bruises, discoloration or wilting.

- Remove roots and stems, if necessary, and any brown or wilted spots.

- To store, line a resealable food-storage plastic bag or tightly-covered container with damp (not wet) paper towels. Place unwashed greens in the bag, and refrigerate up to 5 days. Iceberg lettuce should be rinsed before storing; remove the core and rinse core side up under cold water, then turn upside down to drain. Store as directed for other greens.

- When ready to use greens, rinse under cold water and shake off excess moisture.

- Dry salad greens as much as possible so dressings cling to the leaves and don't become watery. To dry greens, use a salad spinner or place them on a clean kitchen towel or several layers of paper towels, and pat gently to dry.

- Once dry, greens can be stored gently rolled up in the towel or paper towels and placed in a resealable food-storage plastic bag for up to 8 hours.

Tips for Tossed Salads

- Mix mild-flavored greens with more assertive ones. Try tossing butterhead with mesclun, or red chard with romaine and iceberg lettuces. For little dashes of flavor, add fresh herbs!

- Tear greens with your fingers into bite size pieces—don't cut them. Greens go limp and the edges darken if cut with a knife. If you do use a knife, cut up the greens just before serving or use a serrated plastic salad knife (sold in the utensils/gadgets section in large department or discount stores).

- Tomatoes are watery, so wait until just before tossing to add slices, or place them on top of a salad so they won't dilute the dressing or cause the greens to get soggy. Seeding the tomatoes first also helps.

- Add dressing to greens just before serving so they won't get soggy. When "dressing" greens, or tossing with a dressing, start with a small amount, using only enough to lightly coat the leaves, then toss. Or serve the dressing on the side so each person can dress their own. Salads that have been tossed with dressing don't make good leftovers because the salad will become soggy.

- As a rule, stronger greens need a stronger-flavored dressing and mild-tasting greens need a lighter-tasting dressing.

Best Potato Salad Potatoes

Potato salad lovers know the secret to perfect potato salad—it starts with the potatoes! Round red or round white potatoes are best because they're a waxy variety, holding their shape after cooking. Starchy potatoes (long white), like Idaho and russets, have a fluffy texture after cooking and so can become too soft and mushy for potato salad.

Salad Greens Glossary

Arugula (or Rocket): Has small, slender, dark green leaves similar to radish leaves, and a slightly bitter, peppery mustard flavor. Choose smaller leaves for milder flavor.

Belgian Endive (or French): Has narrow, cupped, cream-colored leaves tinged with green and a slightly bitter flavor.

Butterhead Lettuce (Bibb or Boston): Bibb and Boston belong to the butterhead family and have small rounded heads of soft, tender, buttery leaves and a delicate flavor. Bibb is smaller than Boston but has the same delicate, mild flavor.

Cabbage: Comes in several varieties, each with its own distinct flavor. Green and red cabbage are the most common and readily available. Look for compact heads of waxy, tightly wrapped leaves. Savoy cabbage has crinkled leaves, and Chinese (or napa) cabbage has long, crisp leaves.

Curly Endive: Has frilly, narrow, somewhat prickly leaves with a slightly bitter taste.

Escarole: Is a member of the endive family; has broad, wavy, medium green leaves and a slightly bitter flavor, although it's milder than Belgian or curly endive.

Frisée: Is a member of the chicory family; has slender, curly leaves ranging in color from yellow-white to yellow-green and a slightly bitter flavor.

Greens (beet, chard, collard, dandelion, mustard): All have a strong, biting flavor. Young greens are milder and more tender and can be tossed in salads. Older greens are too bitter for salads and should be cooked for the best flavor.

Iceberg Lettuce (or Crisphead): Has a bland mild flavor and very crisp texture. Look for solid, compact heads with tight leaves that range in color from medium green outer leaves to pale green inner ones.

Kale: Is recognized by its sturdy but frilly leaves that usually are dark green and tinged with shades of blue and purple. A member of the cabbage family, it doesn't form a head, but it does have a mild cabbage taste. Choose young small leaves for the best flavor.

Leaf Lettuce (green, red, oak leaf, salad bowl): Has tender but crisp leaves that don't form tight heads. These leafy bunches have a mild flavor that's more full-bodied than iceberg lettuce.

Mâche (Corn Salad): Has spoon-shaped medium to dark green leaves with velvety texture and a mild, subtly sweet and nutty. Also called field salad, field lettuce and lamb's lettuce.

Mesclun (field or wild greens): Is a mixture of young, small greens often including arugula, chervil, chickweed, dandelion, frisée, mizuma and oak leaf lettuce.

Mixed Salad Greens (prepackaged): Are already cleaned and ready to use, you'll find these in the produce section of your supermarket. Choose from a variety of available of mixes, each with its own combination of colors, flavors and textures.

Radicchio: Looks like a small, loose-leaf cabbage; has smooth, tender leaves and a slightly bitter flavor. The two most common radicchios in the United States are a ruby red variety with broad, white veins and one with leaves speckled in shades of pink, red and green.

Romaine (or Cos): Has narrow, elongated, dark green, crisp leaves sometimes tinged with red on the tips. The broad white center rib is especially crunchy.

Sorrel (or Sourgrass): Looks much like spinach, but the leaves are smaller; has a sharp, lemony flavor.

Spinach: Has smooth, tapered, dark green leaves, sometimes with crumpling at the edges, and a slightly bitter flavor.

Watercress: Has small, crisp, dark green, coinsize leaves and a strong peppery flavor.

Caesar Salad

Greek Salad

Gorgonzola and Toasted Walnut Salad

Mandarin Salad

Cold Cucumber Salad

Old-Fashioned Coleslaw

Classic Crunchy Coleslaw

Sweet-Sour Coleslaw

Chinese Cabbage Salad with Sesame Dressing

Perfection Salad

Roasted Beet Salad

Broccoli Sunshine Salad

Peas and Cheese Salad

Country Potato Salad

Classic Creamy Potato Salad

Hot German Potato Salad

Spinach-Strawberry Salad

Cranberry-Raspberry Salad

Apple-Pear Salad

Peach and Plum Salad

Key West Fruit Salad

Avocado-Citrus Salad

1

vegetable and fruit salads

Caesar Salad

Prep Time: 15 min ▪ Start to Finish: 15 min ▪ 6 servings

1 clove garlic, cut in half
8 anchovy fillets, cut up*
1/3 cup olive or vegetable oil
3 tablespoons lemon juice
1 teaspoon Worcestershire sauce
1/4 teaspoon salt
1/4 teaspoon ground mustard
Freshly ground pepper
1 large or 2 small bunches romaine lettuce,
    torn into bite-size pieces (10 cups)
1 cup garlic-flavored croutons
1/3 cup grated Parmesan cheese

1 Rub large wooden salad bowl with cut clove of garlic. Allow a few small pieces of garlic to remain in bowl if desired.

2 In salad bowl, mix anchovies, oil, lemon juice, Worcestershire sauce, salt, mustard and pepper.

3 Add romaine; toss until coated. Sprinkle with croutons and cheese; toss. Serve immediately.

*2 teaspoons anchovy paste can be substituted for the anchovy fillets.

1 Serving (about 1³/₄ cups): Calories 195 (Calories from Fat 145); Total Fat 16g (Saturated Fat 3g); Cholesterol 10mg; Sodium 500mg; Total Carbohydrate 7g (Dietary Fiber 2g); Protein 6g

Greek Salad

Prep Time: 20 min ■ Start to Finish: 20 min ■ 8 servings

Lemon Dressing

1/4 cup vegetable oil

2 tablespoons lemon juice

1/2 teaspoon sugar

11/2 teaspoons Dijon mustard

1/4 teaspoon salt

1/8 teaspoon pepper

Salad

7 oz washed fresh spinach leaves, torn into bite-size pieces (5 cups)

1 head Boston lettuce, torn into bite-size pieces (4 cups)

1 package (4 oz) crumbled feta cheese (1 cup)

4 medium green onions, sliced (1/4 cup)

24 pitted ripe olives

3 medium tomatoes, cut into wedges

1 medium cucumber, sliced

1 In tightly-covered container, shake all dressing ingredients.

2 In large bowl, toss salad ingredients and dressing. Serve immediately.

1 Serving (about 13/4 cups): Calories 140 (Calories from Fat 100); Total Fat 11g (Saturated Fat 3g); Cholesterol 5mg; Sodium 680mg; Total Carbohydrate 6g (Dietary Fiber 2g); Protein 4g

Gorgonzola and Toasted Walnut Salad

Prep Time: 20 min ▪ Start to Finish: 20 min ▪ 6 servings

Toasted Walnut Dressing

$^1/_3$ cup olive or vegetable oil

$^1/_3$ cup coarsely chopped walnuts, toasted

2 tablespoons lemon juice

1 clove garlic

$^1/_8$ teaspoon salt

Dash of pepper

Salad

1 head radicchio, torn into bite-size pieces (4 cups)

1 head Bibb lettuce, torn into bite-size pieces (4 cups)

$^1/_2$ cup crumbled Gorgonzola or Roquefort cheese (2 oz)

$^1/_2$ cup $^1/_2$-inch pieces fresh chives

$^1/_3$ cup coarsely chopped walnuts, toasted*

1 In blender or food processor, place all dressing ingredients. Cover and blend on high speed about 1 minute or until smooth.

2 In large bowl, toss salad ingredients and dressing. Serve immediately.

*For toasted walnuts, cook over medium heat 5 to 7 minutes, stirring frequently until nuts begin to brown, then stirring constantly until nuts are light brown. Or, bake uncovered 6 to 10 minutes, stirring occasionally until nuts are light brown.

1 Serving: Calories 250 (Calories from Fat 215); Total Fat 24g (Saturated Fat 4g); Cholesterol 5mg; Sodium 230mg; Total Carbohydrate 5g (Dietary Fiber 2g); Protein 5g

Mandarin Salad

Prep Time: 20 min ▪ Start to Finish: 30 min ▪ 6 servings

Sugared Almonds
1/4 cup sliced almonds
4 teaspoons sugar

Sweet-Sour Dressing
1/4 cup vegetable oil
2 tablespoons sugar
2 tablespoons white or cider vinegar
1 tablespoon chopped fresh parsley
1/2 teaspoon salt
Dash of pepper
Dash of red pepper sauce

Salad
1/2 small head lettuce, torn into bite-size pieces (3 cups)
1/2 bunch romaine, torn into bite-size pieces (3 cups)
2 medium stalks celery, chopped (1 cup)
2 medium green onions, thinly sliced (2 tablespoons)
1 can (11 oz) mandarin orange segments, drained

1 In 1-quart saucepan, cook almonds and 1 tablespoon plus 1 teaspoon sugar over low heat about 10 minutes, stirring constantly, until sugar is melted and almonds are coated; cool and break apart.

2 In tightly-covered container, shake all dressing ingredients. Refrigerate until serving.

3 In large bowl, toss salad ingredients, dressing and almonds. Serve immediately.

1 Serving (about 1 1/3 cups): Calories 170 (Calories from Fat 110); Total Fat 12g (Saturated Fat 2g); Cholesterol 0mg; Sodium 220mg; Total Carbohydrate 16g (Dietary Fiber 1g); Protein 2g

Cold Cucumber Salad

Prep Time: 15 min ▪ Start to Finish: 15 min ▪ 12 servings

$^1/_2$ cup sugar

$^1/_3$ cup water

1 teaspoon white pepper

$^1/_2$ teaspoon salt

$1^1/_2$ cups cider vinegar

4 large cucumbers, peeled, thinly sliced

$^1/_4$ cup chopped fresh parsley

1 In medium saucepan, mix sugar, water, white pepper and salt. Heat mixture over medium-high heat to boiling and boil until sugar is dissolved. Remove from heat and cool. Stir in vinegar.

2 Pour mixture over cucumber slices. Sprinkle with parsley. Cover and refrigerate until ready to serve.

1 Serving: Calories 50 (Calories from Fat 0); Total Fat 0g (Saturated Fat 0g); Cholesterol 0mg; Sodium 100mg; Total Carbohydrate 13g (Dietary Fiber 1g); Protein 1g

When the temperature is too hot to handle, try whipping up this cool salad. Even better, you can make it a day ahead of time. This is the perfect side for deli subs or anything hot off the grill.

Old-Fashioned Coleslaw

Prep Time: 25 min ■ Start to Finish: 3 hr 25 min ■ 8 servings

3 tablespoons sugar
2 tablespoons all-purpose flour
1 teaspoon ground mustard
1/2 teaspoon salt
1/8 teaspoon ground red pepper (cayenne)
1 egg
3/4 cup water
1/4 cup lemon juice
1 tablespoon margarine or butter
1/4 cup sour cream
1 lb green cabbage, shredded or finely chopped (6 cups)
1 medium carrot, shredded (1 cup)
1 small bell pepper, finely chopped (1/2 cup)

1 In heavy 1-quart saucepan, mix sugar, flour, mustard, salt and red pepper. Beat in egg. Stir in water and lemon juice gradually until well blended. Cook over low heat 13 to 15 minutes, stirring constantly, until thick and smooth; remove from heat.

2 Stir in margarine until melted. Place plastic wrap directly on surface of dressing and refrigerate about 2 hours or until cool. Stir in sour cream.

3 In large bowl, mix dressing, cabbage, carrot and bell pepper; toss well. Refrigerate at least 1 hour but no longer than 24 hours.

1 Serving: Calories 85 (Calories from Fat 35); Total Fat 4g (Saturated Fat 1g); Cholesterol 30mg; Sodium 190mg; Total Carbohydrate 12g (Dietary Fiber 2g); Protein 2g

Classic Crunchy Coleslaw

Prep Time: 15 min ▪ Start to Finish: 15 min ▪ 8 servings

$1/2$ cup sour cream or plain yogurt
$1/4$ cup mayonnaise or salad dressing
1 teaspoon sugar
$1/2$ teaspoon dry mustard
$1/2$ teaspoon seasoned salt
$1/8$ teaspoon pepper
1 lb green cabbage, finely shredded or chopped (4 cups)
1 small onion, chopped ($1/4$ cup)
Paprika, if desired
Dill weed, if desired

1 In large bowl, mix sour cream, mayonnaise, sugar, mustard, seasoned salt and pepper. Toss with cabbage and onion.

2 Sprinkle with paprika or dried dill weed.

1 Serving: Calories 125 (Calories from Fat 100); Total Fat 11g (Saturated Fat 3g); Cholesterol 20mg; Sodium 180mg; Total Carbohydrate 6g (Dietary Fiber 2g); Protein 2g

This mayonnaise- and sour cream–based recipe for coleslaw is creamy, crunchy and not too sweet. It keeps well for several days in the refrigerator. Just keep it tightly covered.

Sweet-Sour Coleslaw

Prep Time: 20 min ▪ Start to Finish: 20 min ▪ 6 servings

1 egg
¼ cup sugar
¼ cup vinegar
2 tablespoons water
2 tablespoons margarine or butter
1 teaspoon salt
½ teaspoon ground mustard
1 lb green cabbage, finely shredded or chopped (4 cups)
1 small bell pepper, chopped (½ cup)

1 In medium bowl, beat egg until thick and lemon-colored.

2 In 1-qt saucepan, heat sugar, vinegar, water, margarine, salt and mustard to boiling, stirring constantly. Gradually stir at least half of the hot mixture into egg, then stir into hot mixture in saucepan. Cook over low heat about 5 minutes, stirring constantly, until thickened.

3 In large bowl, place cabbage and bell pepper. Pour hot mixture over cabbage and bell pepper; toss. For best flavor, this coleslaw should be covered and refrigerated for 2 to 4 hours before serving.

1 Serving: Calories 80 (Calories from Fat 35); Total Fat 4g (Saturated Fat 1g); Cholesterol 2mg; Sodium 350mg; Total Carbohydrate 10g (Dietary Fiber 1g); Protein 2g

The Pennsylvania Dutch, originally from southern Germany, use a boiled sweet-sour dressing on both coleslaw and potato salad to give them a nice, tangy flavor that goes with the crunch of the cabbage. The secret to their classic boiled dressing is to cook it quickly and not let the eggs clump.

Chinese Cabbage Salad with Sesame Dressing

Prep Time: 15 min ▪ Start to Finish: 15 min ▪ 4 servings

Sesame Dressing
3 tablespoons rice or white wine vinegar
2 teaspoons sugar
2 teaspoons sesame seed, toasted*
2 teaspoons soy sauce
1 teaspoon sesame oil
$\frac{1}{8}$ teaspoon crushed red pepper

Salad
2 cups finely shredded Chinese (napa) cabbage (8 oz)
$\frac{1}{4}$ cup chopped jicama
$\frac{1}{4}$ cup chopped green bell pepper
$\frac{1}{4}$ cup coarsely shredded carrot

1 In tightly-covered container, shake all dressing ingredients.

2 In medium glass or plastic bowl, toss salad ingredients and dressing. Cover and refrigerate until serving time.

*For toasted sesame seeds, cook over medium-low heat 5 to 7 minutes, stirring frequently until browning begins, then stirring constantly until golden brown. Or, bake 8 to 10 minutes, stirring occasionally until golden brown.

1 Serving: Calories 60 (Calories from Fat 20); Total Fat 2g (Saturated Fat 0g); Cholesterol 0mg; Sodium 170mg; Total Carbohydrate 9g (Dietary Fiber 2g); Protein 1g

Perfection Salad

Prep Time: 15 min ▮ Start to Finish: 3 hr 15 min ▮ 6 servings

1 cup boiling water
1 package (4-serving size) lemon-flavored gelatin
1 cup cold water
2 tablespoons lemon juice or vinegar
1 teaspoon salt
1 cup finely diced celery
1 cup finely shredded green cabbage
1/3 cup chopped sweet pickles
2 tablespoons finely chopped pimientos

1 Pour boiling water on gelatin in 2-quart bowl; stir until gelatin is dissolved. Stir in cold water, lemon juice and salt. Refrigerate until slightly thickened but not set.

2 Stir in remaining ingredients. Pour into 4-cup mold or 6 individual molds. Refrigerate until firm; unmold.

1 Serving: Calories 30 (Calories from Fat 0); Total Fat 0g (Saturated Fat 0g); Cholesterol 0mg; Sodium 516mg; Total Carbohydrate 7g (Dietary Fiber 7g); Protein 1g

Roasted Beet Salad

Prep Time: 15 min ▪ Start to Finish: 1 hr 25 min ▪ 4 servings

1½ lb small beets (1½ to 2 inches in diameter)
4 cups bite-size pieces mixed salad greens
1 medium orange, peeled, sliced
½ cup walnut halves, toasted,* coarsely chopped
¼ cup crumbled chèvre (goat) cheese
½ cup Fresh Herb Vinaigrette (page 152)

1 Heat oven to 425°F. Remove greens from beets, leaving about ½ inch of stem. Wash beets well; leave whole with root ends attached. Place beets in ungreased 13 × 9-inch pan; drizzle with oil. Bake uncovered about 40 minutes or until tender.

2 Remove skins from beets under running water. Let beets cool until easy to handle, about 30 minutes. Peel beets and cut off root ends; cut beets into slices. Cut each slice in half.

3 On 4 salad plates, arrange salad greens. Top with beets, orange slices, walnuts and cheese. Serve with Fresh Herb Vinaigrette.

*For toasted walnuts, cook over medium heat 5 to 7 minutes, stirring frequently until nuts begin to brown, then stirring constantly until nuts are light brown. Or, bake uncovered 6 to 10 minutes, stirring occasionally until nuts are light brown.

1 Serving: Calories 320 (Calories from Fat 250); Total Fat 28g (Saturated Fat 5g); Cholesterol 5mg; Sodium 280mg; Total Carbohydrate 16g (Dietary Fiber 5g); Protein 7g

Broccoli Sunshine Salad

Prep Time: 15 min ▪ Start to Finish: 15 min ▪ 6 servings

$^1/_2$ cup mayonnaise or salad dressing

1 tablespoon sugar

2 tablespoons cider vinegar

3 cups broccoli florets ($^1/_2$ lb)

$^1/_3$ cup raisins

$^1/_4$ cup shredded Cheddar cheese (1 oz)

4 slices bacon, crisply cooked and crumbled ($^1/_4$ cup)

2 tablespoons chopped red onion

1 In large glass or plastic bowl, mix mayonnaise, sugar and vinegar.

2 Add remaining ingredients; toss until evenly coated. Store covered in refrigerator.

1 Serving (about $^1/_2$ cup): Calories 220 (Calories from Fat 160); Total Fat 18g (Saturated Fat 4g); Cholesterol 20mg; Sodium 210mg; Total Carbohydrate 12g (Dietary Fiber 2g); Protein 4g

Stir this salad just before serving to redistribute all the ingredients. If the dressing is too thick, thin it with a little milk.

Peas and Cheese Salad

Prep Time: 10 min ▪ Start to Finish: 1 hr 10 min ▪ 6 servings

1/3 to 1/2 cup mayonnaise or salad dressing
1/2 teaspoon salt
1/2 teaspoon yellow mustard
1/4 teaspoon sugar
1/8 teaspoon pepper
2 cups cooked shelled fresh green peas
1 cup diced mild Cheddar or Colby cheese
1 medium stalk celery, thinly sliced (1/2 cup)
3 sweet pickles, chopped (1/4 cup)
2 tablespoons finely chopped onion
2 hard-cooked eggs, chopped
Lettuce leaves, if desired

1 In 2½ quart bowl, mix mayonnaise, salt, mustard, sugar and pepper.

2 Add peas, cheese, celery, pickles and onion; toss. Stir in eggs. Cover and refrigerate at least 1 hour or until chilled. Serve on lettuce leaves. Immediately refrigerate any remaining salad.

1 Serving: Calories 240 (Calories from Fat 160); Total Fat 18g (Saturated Fat 6g); Cholesterol 100mg; Sodium 500mg; Total Carbohydrate 10g (Dietary Fiber 3g); Protein 9g

Kidney Bean and Cheese Salad: Substitute 1 can (15 oz) kidney beans, rinsed, drained, for the fresh green peas.

Country Potato Salad

Prep Time: 10 min ▪ Start to Finish: 4 hr 45 min ▪ 10 servings

Salad	Cooked Salad Dressing
2 lb peeled potatoes (6 medium)	2 tablespoons all-purpose flour
¼ cup Italian dressing	1 tablespoon sugar
2 medium stalks celery, sliced	1 teaspoon ground mustard
(1 cup)	¾ teaspoon salt
1 medium cucumber, chopped	¼ teaspoon pepper
(1 cup)	1 egg yolk, slightly beaten
1 large onion, chopped (1 cup)	¾ cup milk
6 radishes, thinly sliced (½ cup)	2 tablespoons vinegar
4 hard-cooked eggs, chopped	1 tablespoon margarine or butter

1 In 3-qt saucepan, heat 1 inch water (salted, if desired) to boiling. Add potatoes. Cover and heat to boiling; reduce heat. Cook 30 to 35 minutes or until tender. Drain and cool slightly.

2 Cut potatoes into cubes (about 6 cups). In 4-quart glass or plastic bowl, toss warm potatoes with Italian dressing. Cover and refrigerate at least 4 hours.

3 Meanwhile, in 1-quart saucepan, mix flour, sugar, mustard, salt and pepper. In small bowl, mix egg yolk and milk and slowly stir into flour mixture. Cook over medium heat, stirring constantly, until mixture thickens and boils. Boil and stir 1 minute; remove from heat. Stir in vinegar and margarine. Place plastic wrap directly on surface. Refrigerate until cool, at least 1 hour.

4 Add celery, cucumber, onion, radishes and eggs to potatoes. Pour salad dressing over top and toss. Refrigerate until chilled. Immediately refrigerate any remaining salad.

1 Serving: Calories 290 (Calories from Fat 200); Fat 22g (Saturated Fat 4g); Cholesterol 100mg; Sodium 210mg; Total Carbohydrate 20g (Dietary Fiber 2g); Protein 5g

Classic Creamy Potato Salad

Prep Time: 10 min ■ Start to Finish: 4 hr 45 min ■ 10 servings

2 lb boiling potatoes (6 medium)
1½ cups mayonnaise or salad dressing
1 tablespoon vinegar
1 tablespoon yellow mustard
1 teaspoon salt
¼ teaspoon pepper
2 medium stalks celery, chopped (1 cup)
1 medium onion, chopped (½ cup)
4 hard-cooked eggs, chopped

1 In 3-qt saucepan, heat 1 inch water (salted, if desired) to boiling. Add potatoes. Cover and heat to boiling; reduce heat to low. Boil gently 30 to 35 minutes or until potatoes are tender; drain and cool slightly. Cut into cubes (about 6 cups).

2 In large glass or plastic bowl, mix mayonnaise, vinegar, mustard, salt and pepper. Add potatoes, celery and onion; toss. Stir in eggs. Cover and refrigerate at least 4 hours. Cover and refrigerate any remaining salad.

1 Serving: Calories 350 (Calories from Fat 250); Total Fat 28g (Saturated Fat 5g); Cholesterol 105mg; Sodium 480mg; Total Carbohydrate 21g (Dietary Fiber 2g); Protein 5g

Create a picnic anywhere, anytime, with this creamy potato salad. For a summery flavor and a cool crunch, stir in ½ cup each thinly sliced radishes, chopped cucumber and chopped bell pepper.

Hot German Potato Salad

Prep Time: 30 min ▪ Start to Finish: 1 hr 5 min ▪ 5 servings

1½ lb potatoes (4 medium)
3 slices bacon
1 medium onion, chopped (½ cup)
1 tablespoon all-purpose flour
1 tablespoon sugar
1 teaspoon salt
¼ teaspoon celery seed
Dash of pepper
½ cup water
¼ cup vinegar

1 In 3-qt saucepan, heat 1 inch water (salted if desired) to boiling. Add potatoes. Cover and heat to boiling; reduce heat. Cook 30 to 35 minutes or until tender; drain. Cut into thin slices and keep warm.

2 In 8-inch skillet, cook bacon until crisp; remove bacon and drain.

3 Cook and stir onion in bacon fat until tender. Stir in flour, sugar, salt, celery seed and pepper. Cook over low heat, stirring constantly, until bubbly; remove from heat. Stir in water and vinegar. Heat to boiling, stirring constantly. Boil and stir 1 minute; remove from heat.

4 Crumble bacon into hot mixture, then add warm potatoes. Cook, stirring gently to coat potato slices, until hot and bubbly.

1 Serving: Calories 199 (Calories from Fat 57); Total Fat 2g (Saturated Fat 2g); Cholesterol 9mg; Sodium 587mg; Total Carbohydrate 31g (Dietary Fiber 2g); Protein 5g

Spinach-Strawberry Salad

Prep Time: 20 min ▪ Start to Finish: 20 min ▪ 4 servings

Honey-Dijon Dressing
2 tablespoons vegetable oil
2 tablespoons honey
2 tablespoons orange juice
1 tablespoon cider vinegar or white vinegar
1 teaspoon poppy seed, if desired
2 teaspoons Dijon mustard

Salad
1 small jicama, peeled, cut into 1 x ¼-inch sticks (about ¾ cup)
2 kiwifruit, sliced
½ pint (1 cup) fresh strawberries
8 cups ready-to-eat spinach (from 9- or 10-oz bag)

1 In tightly-covered container, shake all dressing ingredients.

2 In large salad bowl, place spinach, strawberries, jicama and kiwifruit. Shake dressing again to mix ingredients. Pour over salad; toss. Serve immediately.

1 Serving: Calories 190 (Calories from Fat 70); Total Fat 8g (Saturated Fat 1g); Cholesterol 0mg; Sodium 115mg; Total Carbohydrate 28g (Dietary Fiber 7g); Protein 3g

Leftover jicama can be cut into sticks and served with other raw vegetables for a snack or appetizer. Packaged mixed salad greens that are already cleaned and ready to use are available in the produce section of the supermarket and can be used instead of the spinach. A 10-ounce bag is about 7 cups of greens. The Italian variety is especially pretty.

Cranberry-Raspberry Salad

Prep Time: 10 min ▪ Start to Finish: 12 hr 10 min ▪ 12 servings

2 packages (12 oz each) cranberry-orange sauce
1 package (12 oz) cranberry-raspberry sauce
1 package (6 oz) lemon-flavored gelatin
2 cups boiling water
Watercress, if desired
Cranberries, if desired

1 Lightly oil 6½-cup ring mold.

2 In large bowl, mix cranberry sauces together. Dissolve gelatin in boiling water and stir into cranberry sauces. Pour into mold. Cover and refrigerate overnight.

3 Unmold salad on serving plate. Garnish with watercress and cranberries.

1 Serving: Calories 190 (Calories from Fat 0); Total Fat 0g (Saturated Fat 0g); Cholesterol 0mg; Sodium 60mg; Total Carbohydrate 49g (Dietary Fiber 2g); Protein 1g

The tang of cranberry and the fruity coolness of the lemon gelatin make this salad a hit at any meal. It's sure to become a family favorite at the Thanksgiving table.

Apple-Pear Salad

Prep Time: 25 min ■ Start to Finish: 25 min ■ 8 servings

1 large red apple, cut into fourths, then cut crosswise into thin slices
1 large pear, cut into fourths, then cut crosswise into thin slices
1 medium stalk celery, cut diagonally into thin slices (¹/₂ cup)
4 oz Havarti cheese, cut into julienne strips
3 tablespoons olive or vegetable oil
2 tablespoons frozen (thawed) apple juice concentrate
3 tablespoons coarsely chopped honey-roasted peanuts

1 In medium salad bowl, mix apple, pear, celery and cheese.

2 In small bowl, thoroughly mix oil and juice concentrate. Pour over apple mixture and toss to coat. Sprinkle with peanuts.

1 Serving: Calories 150 (Calories from Fat 100); Total Fat 11g (Saturated Fat 4g); Cholesterol 15mg; Sodium 110mg; Total Carbohydrate 10g (Dietary Fiber 1g); Protein 3g

Peach and Plum Salad

Prep Time: 10 min ▪ Start to Finish: 10 min ▪ 6 servings

3 medium plums, sliced
3 medium peaches, sliced
$1/2$ cup coarsely chopped walnuts, toasted*
$1/4$ cup raspberry preserves
2 tablespoons red wine vinegar or white vinegar
1 tablespoon vegetable oil

1 Arrange plums and peaches on serving plate. Sprinkle with walnuts.

2 In small bowl, mix remaining ingredients and drizzle over fruit.

*For toasted walnuts, cook over medium heat 5 to 7 minutes, stirring frequently until nuts begin to brown, then stirring constantly until nuts are light brown. Or, bake uncovered 6 to 10 minutes, stirring occasionally until nuts are light brown.

1 Serving: Calories 170 (Calories from Fat 80); Total Fat 9g (Saturated Fat 1g); Cholesterol 0mg; Sodium 5mg; Total Carbohydrate 21g (Dietary Fiber 2g); Protein 2g

Key West Fruit Salad

Prep Time: 25 min ▪ Start to Finish: 2 hr 25 min ▪ 8 servings

3/4 cup sugar

1/4 cup water

1/4 cup fresh or bottled Key lime juice or regular lime juice

2 to 3 tablespoons tequila or Key lime juice

1 teaspoon grated Key lime peel or regular lime peel

14 cups cut-up fresh fruit (such as pineapple, strawberries, kiwifruit or grapes)

1 In 1½-quart saucepan, heat sugar and water to boiling; reduce heat. Simmer uncovered about 2 minutes, stirring constantly, until sugar is dissolved. Remove from heat. Stir in lime juice and tequila.

2 Let lime dressing stand until room temperature. Cover and refrigerate about 2 hours or until cool.

3 Stir lime peel into dressing. In very large bowl, carefully toss fruit and dressing. Serve immediately.

1 Serving: Calories 65 (Calories from Fat 0); Total Fat 0g (Saturated Fat 0g); Cholesterol 0mg; Sodium 5mg; Total Carbohydrate 16g (Dietary Fiber 2g); Protein 1g

This salad makes about 14 cups, so it's perfect for potlucks, open houses, graduations and showers as well as brunches.

Avocado-Citrus Salad

Prep Time: 10 min ▪ Start to Finish: 10 min ▪ 4 servings

2 tablespoons lime juice
2 tablespoons olive oil
1 tablespoon chopped fresh mint leaves
Lettuce leaves
2 small avocados, sliced
1 grapefruit, peeled, sliced
1 large orange, peeled, sliced
1 small red onion, chopped ($\frac{1}{4}$ cup)

1 In small bowl, mix lime juice, olive oil and mint; set aside.

2 Line 4 salad plates with lettuce. Arrange avocado, grapefruit and orange slices on lettuce. Sprinkle with red onion. Drizzle with lime juice mixture.

1 Serving: Calories 270 (Calories from Fat 184); Total Fat 20g (Saturated 3g); Cholesterol 0mg; Sodium 9mg; Total Carbohydrate 23g (Dietary Fiber 10g); Protein 3g

Northern Italian White Bean Salad

Warm Tuscan Bean Salad

Heartland Three-Bean Salad

Corn and Black Bean Salad

Veggies and Kasha with Balsamic Vinaigrette

Creamy Rice-Fruit Salad

Turkey–Wild Rice Salad

Harvest Salad

Wheat Berry Salad

Creamy Quinoa Primavera

Mediterranean Quinoa Salad

Red Harvest Quinoa

Tabbouleh

Tarragon-Couscous Salad

Mediterranean Couscous Salad

2

bean and whole grain salads

Northern Italian
White Bean Salad

Prep Time: 15 min ▮ Start to Finish: 2hr 15 min ▮ 6 servings

2 cans (19 oz each) cannellini beans, rinsed, drained
1 large tomato, seeded, coarsely chopped (1 cup)
1 small red bell pepper, chopped ($\frac{1}{2}$ cup)
$\frac{1}{2}$ cup chopped red onion
$\frac{1}{4}$ cup chopped fresh parsley
$\frac{1}{4}$ cup olive or vegetable oil
2 tablespoons chopped fresh or 2 teaspoons dried basil leaves
2 tablespoons red wine vinegar
$\frac{1}{2}$ teaspoon salt
$\frac{1}{8}$ teaspoon pepper
12 lettuce leaves

1 In large glass or plastic bowl, carefully mix all ingredients except lettuce.

2 Cover and refrigerate at least 2 hours to blend flavors. Just before serving, spoon onto lettuce, using slotted spoon.

1 Serving: Calories 300 (Calories from Fat 90); Total Fat 10g (Saturated Fat 1g); Cholesterol 0mg; Sodium 210mg; Total Carbohydrate 48g (Dietary Fiber 13g); Protein 18g

Warm Tuscan Bean Salad

Prep Time: 30 min ▪ Start to Finish: 30 min ▪ 4 servings

1 tablespoon olive or vegetable oil

2 medium carrots, sliced (1 cup)

1 medium onion, chopped ($\frac{1}{2}$ cup)

2 cans (15 to 19 oz each) cannellini beans, drained, $\frac{1}{2}$ cup liquid reserved

$1\frac{1}{2}$ teaspoons chopped fresh or $\frac{1}{2}$ teaspoon dried oregano leaves

$\frac{1}{4}$ teaspoon pepper

4 cups bite-size pieces spinach leaves

$\frac{1}{4}$ cup red wine vinaigrette or Italian dressing

2 tablespoons bacon flavor bits

1 In 12-inch skillet, heat oil over medium heat. Add carrots and onion; cook 5 to 7 minutes, stirring occasionally, until vegetables are crisp-tender.

2 Stir in beans, ½ cup reserved liquid, the oregano and pepper. Cook 5 minutes, stirring occasionally.

3 Line large platter with spinach. Top with bean mixture. Pour vinaigrette over salad; sprinkle with bacon bits.

1 Serving: Calories 330 (Calories from Fat 70); Total Fat 7g (Saturated Fat 1g); Cholesterol 0mg; Sodium 680mg; Total Carbohydrate 49g (Dietary Fiber 13g); Protein 17g

Warm Tuscan Bean and Chicken Salad: Omit 1 can of cannellini beans. Add 1½ cups cubed cooked chicken or turkey with the beans in step 2.

Heartland Three-Bean Salad

Prep Time: 15 min ▮ Start to Finish: 3 hr 15 min ▮ 12 servings

1 can (16 oz) cut green beans, drained
1 can (16 oz) cut wax beans, drained
1 can (15 oz) kidney beans, drained
1 cup thinly sliced onion, cut in half
1 small bell pepper, finely chopped ($^{1}/_{2}$ cup)
2 tablespoons chopped fresh parsley
$^{2}/_{3}$ cup vinegar
$^{1}/_{2}$ cup sugar
$^{1}/_{3}$ cup vegetable oil
$^{1}/_{2}$ teaspoon pepper
$^{1}/_{2}$ teaspoon salt
2 slices bacon, crisply cooked, crumbled

1 In 3-quart bowl, mix beans, onion, bell pepper and parsley.

2 In 1½-quart saucepan, mix remaining ingredients except bacon. Heat to boiling, stirring occasionally. Pour over beans; stir.

3 Cover and refrigerate, stirring occasionally, at least 3 hours or until chilled. Just before serving, sprinkle with bacon.

1 Serving: Calories 160 (Calories from Fat 65); Total Fat 7g (Saturated Fat 1g); Cholesterol 0mg; Sodium 400mg; Total Carbohydrate 23g (Dietary Fiber 4g); Protein 5g

Corn and Black Bean Salad

Prep Time: 5 min ▪ Start to Finish: 2 hr 5 min ▪ 6 servings

1 can (15 ounces) black beans, rinsed and drained
1 can (about 8 ounces) whole kernel corn, drained
1 can (4 ounces) chopped green chilies, drained
$\frac{1}{2}$ cup medium chunky-style salsa
$\frac{1}{4}$ cup chopped onion
2 tablespoons chopped fresh cilantro

1 In medium bowl, mix all ingredients.

2 Cover and refrigerate at least 2 hours but no longer than 24 hours.

1 Serving ($\frac{1}{2}$ cup each): Calories 135 (Calories from Fat 10); Total Fat 1g (Saturated Fat 0g); Cholesterol 0mg; Sodium 760mg; Total Carbohydrate 29g (Dietary Fiber 6g); Protein 8g

Veggies and Kasha with Balsamic Vinaigrette

Prep Time: 15 min ▪ Start to Finish: 2 hr 20 min ▪ 4 servings

Salad

1 cup water
$1/2$ cup uncooked buckwheat kernels or groats (kasha)
4 medium green onions, thinly sliced ($1/4$ cup)
2 medium tomatoes, seeded, coarsely chopped ($1^1/2$ cups)
1 medium unpeeled cucumber, seeded, chopped ($1^1/4$ cups)

Vinaigrette

2 tablespoons balsamic or red wine vinegar
1 tablespoon olive oil
2 teaspoons sugar
$1/2$ teaspoon salt
$1/4$ teaspoon pepper
1 clove garlic, finely chopped

1 In 8-inch skillet, heat water to boiling. Add kasha; cook over medium-high heat 7 to 8 minutes, stirring occasionally, until tender. Drain if necessary.

2 In large bowl, mix kasha and remaining salad ingredients.

3 In tightly-covered container, shake all vinaigrette ingredients until blended. Pour vinaigrette over kasha mixture; toss. Cover; refrigerate 1 to 2 hours to blend flavors.

1 Serving: Calories 120 (Calories from Fat 35); Total Fat 4g (Saturated Fat 0.5g); Cholesterol 0mg; Sodium 300mg; Total Carbohydrate 18g (Dietary Fiber 3g); Protein 3g

The color and crunch of the vegetables and the chewiness of the kasha create a salad that looks and tastes wonderful, perfect for family and friends.

Creamy Rice-Fruit Salad

Prep Time: 15 min ▌ Start to Finish: 1 hr 15 min ▌ 8 servings

$^2/_3$ cup uncooked wild rice

$1^2/_3$ cups water

1 container (8 oz) lemon or orange low-fat yogurt

1 tablespoon honey

1 cup fresh strawberries, cut in half

$^1/_2$ cup seedless green grapes, cut in half

1 kiwifruit, peeled, cut into $^1/_4$-inch slices, slices cut into quarters

1 medium seedless orange, cut into 1-inch pieces (1 cup)

1 teaspoon chopped fresh or $^1/_4$ teaspoon dried mint leaves

1 Cook wild rice in water as directed on package. Place cooked wild rice in colander or strainer; rinse with cold water 5 minutes to chill.

2 In medium bowl, mix yogurt and honey. Add cooked wild rice and remaining ingredients; toss.

1 Serving: Calories 120 (Calories from Fat 5); Total Fat 0.5g (Saturated Fat 0g); Cholesterol 0mg; Sodium 20mg; Total Carbohydrate 24g (Dietary Fiber 2g); Protein 4g

If you like brown rice, you can substitute that for the wild rice. Or use a combination of brown rice and wild rice for a great taste and appearance.

Turkey–Wild Rice Salad

Prep Time: 20 min ▪ Start to Finish: 1 hr 20 min ▪ 4 servings

1 cup uncooked wild rice
2½ cups water
1 lb uncooked turkey breast slices, about ¼ inch thick
¼ teaspoon seasoned salt
¼ teaspoon dried marjoram leaves
¼ cup chopped walnuts
¼ cup sweetened dried cranberries
4 medium green onions, chopped (¼ cup)
¼ teaspoon salt
½ cup fresh raspberries
4 large leaf lettuce leaves
½ cup raspberry vinaigrette dressing

1 Cook wild rice in water as directed on package. Place cooked wild rice in colander or strainer; rinse with cold water 5 minutes to chill.

2 Sprinkle turkey with seasoned salt and marjoram. Spray 10-inch skillet with cooking spray; heat over medium-high heat. Cook turkey in skillet 4 to 6 minutes, turning once, until no longer pink in center. Cut into 2-inch pieces.

3 In large bowl, mix cooked wild rice, walnuts, cranberries, onions and salt. Carefully stir in raspberries.

4 On 4 plates, arrange lettuce leaves. Top with rice mixture. Arrange warm turkey on rice mixture. Drizzle with dressing.

1 Serving: Calories 390 (Calories from Fat 60); Total Fat 7g (Saturated Fat 1g); Cholesterol 75mg; Sodium 650mg; Total Carbohydrate 48g (Dietary Fiber 5g); Protein 34g

Make it easier on yourself by preparing the wild rice one night and letting it chill, then adding the rest of the ingredients the next night when you serve this salad.

Harvest Salad

Prep Time: 20 min ▪ Start to Finish: 40 min ▪ 8 servings

1 cup uncooked quick-cooking barley
2 cups water
2 cups frozen whole kernel corn (from 1-lb bag), thawed, drained
$^1/_2$ cup sweetened dried cranberries
4 medium green onions, thinly sliced ($^1/_4$ cup)
1 medium unpeeled apple, chopped (1 cup)
1 small carrot, coarsely shredded ($^1/_3$ cup)
2 tablespoons canola oil
2 tablespoons honey
1 tablespoon lemon juice

1 Cook barley in water as directed on package.

2 In large bowl, mix cooked barley, corn, cranberries, onions, apple and carrot.

3 In tightly-covered container, shake oil, honey and lemon juice. Pour over barley mixture; toss.

1 Serving: Calories 240 (Calories from Fat 40); Total Fat 4g (Saturated Fat 0g); Cholesterol 0mg; Sodium 10mg; Total Carbohydrate 45g (Dietary Fiber 7g); Protein 4g

Quick-cooking barley contains the nutrients of regular barley in a convenient, time-saving form. Combining grains, fruits and vegetables makes an interesting and good-for-you salad, one that's colorful and fancy enough to serve to company, yet easy enough to make for just you and your family.

Wheat Berry Salad

Prep Time: 10 min ▪ Start to Finish: 2 hr 40 min ▪ 8 servings

Wheat Berries

1 cup uncooked wheat berries

4 cups water

Creamy Vinaigrette Dressing

1/3 cup canola oil

2 tablespoons mayonnaise or salad dressing

2 tablespoons red wine vinegar

1/2 teaspoon salt

1/4 teaspoon garlic powder

1/8 teaspoon pepper

Salad

1 cup chopped broccoli

1 cup chopped cauliflower

1 cup cherry tomatoes, cut in half

1 small green bell pepper, chopped (1/2 cup)

4 medium green onions, sliced (1/4 cup)

1/2 cup crumbled reduced-fat feta cheese (2 oz)

1 In 3-quart saucepan, soak wheat berries in water 30 minutes. Heat to boiling over high heat. Reduce heat to low. Partially cover; simmer 55 to 60 minutes or until wheat berries are tender. Drain and rinse with cold water.

2 In small bowl, stir all dressing ingredients until well mixed.

3 In large serving bowl, toss wheat berries, salad ingredients and dressing. Cover; refrigerate at least 1 hour.

1 Serving: Calories 190 (Calories from Fat 120); Total Fat 13g (Saturated Fat 2g); Cholesterol 0mg; Sodium 280mg; Total Carbohydrate 14g (Dietary Fiber 3g); Protein 4g

Wheat berries are whole, unprocessed kernels of wheat. Look for wheat berries in the cereal, self-serve bulk foods or natural-foods section of your supermarket.

Creamy Quinoa Primavera

Prep Time: 20 min ▪ Start to Finish: 35 min ▪ 6 servings

1¹/₂ cups uncooked quinoa

3 cups chicken broth

2 teaspoons canola oil

2 cloves garlic, finely chopped

5 cups assorted vegetables, thinly sliced or bite-size pieces
     (such as asparagus, broccoli, carrot and zucchini)

3 oz (from 8-oz package)

¹/₃-less-fat cream cheese (Neufchâtel)

1 tablespoon chopped fresh or 1 teaspoon dried basil leaves

2 tablespoons grated Romano cheese

1 In colander or strainer, rinse quinoa thoroughly; drain. In 2-quart saucepan, heat quinoa and broth to boiling; reduce heat. Cover; simmer 10 to 15 minutes or until all broth is absorbed.

2 Meanwhile, in 12-inch nonstick skillet, heat oil over medium-high heat. Cook garlic in oil about 30 seconds, stirring frequently, until golden. Stir in vegetables. Cook about 5 minutes, stirring frequently, until vegetables are crisp-tender.

3 Stir cream cheese and basil into quinoa. Add quinoa mixture to vegetables; toss. Sprinkle with Romano cheese.

1 Serving: Calories 270 (Calories from Fat 80); Total Fat 9g (Saturated Fat 3g); Cholesterol 15mg; Sodium 620mg; Total Carbohydrate 34g (Dietary Fiber 4g); Protein 12g

One technique to add more flavor to grains is to cook and stir them in a little butter or oil on the stove-top. This "toasts" the grain, so the flavors pop more. You can try that in this dish: Drain the quinoa, cook and stir it in a little melted butter for a few minutes, then add the rest of the ingredients.

Mediterranean Quinoa Salad

Prep Time: 30 min ▪ Start to Finish: 1 hr 35 min ▪ 4 servings

1 cup uncooked quinoa

2 cups roasted garlic–seasoned chicken broth (from two 14-oz cans)

$1/2$ cup chopped drained roasted red bell peppers (from 7-oz jar)

$1/2$ cup cubed provolone cheese

$1/4$ cup chopped kalamata olives

2 tablespoons chopped fresh basil leaves

2 tablespoons Italian dressing

1 Rinse quinoa thoroughly by placing in a fine-mesh strainer and holding under cold running water until water runs clear; drain well.

2 In 2-quart saucepan, heat quinoa and broth to boiling; reduce heat. Cover; simmer 15 to 20 minutes or until quinoa is tender. Drain quinoa. Cool completely, about 45 minutes.

3 In large serving bowl, toss quinoa and remaining ingredients. Serve immediately, or refrigerate 1 to 2 hours before serving.

1 Serving: Calories 290 (Calories from Fat 100); Total Fat 12g (Saturated Fat 3.5g); Cholesterol 15mg; Sodium 810mg; Total Carbohydrate 33g (Dietary Fiber 3g); Protein 13g

Quinoa is a popular grain in South American cuisine and is gaining popularity in the United States. Its nutrition profile is impressive because it is a complete protein.

Red Harvest Quinoa

Prep Time: 20 min   Start to Finish: 40 min   8 servings

1 cup uncooked red or white quinoa
1 tablespoon butter or margarine
$1/4$ cup chopped red onion
$1/3$ cup chopped celery
$1/2$ cup coarsely chopped baking apple
$1^1/_2$ cups roasted vegetable stock (from 32-oz container) or chicken broth
$1/2$ cup orange juice
$1/2$ cup sweetened dried cranberries
1 jar (1.75 oz) pine nuts (about $1/3$ cup), toasted*
$1/4$ cup shredded Parmesan cheese (1 oz)
$1/4$ teaspoon salt
2 tablespoons finely chopped parsley

1 Rinse quinoa thoroughly by placing in a fine-mesh strainer and holding under cold running water until water runs clear; drain well.

2 In 2-quart saucepan, melt butter over medium heat. Cook onion, celery, apple and quinoa in butter 5 minutes, stirring occasionally.

3 Stir in vegetable stock and orange juice. Heat to boiling; reduce heat. Cover; simmer 15 to 20 minutes or until all liquid is absorbed and quinoa is tender. Fluff with fork.

4 Stir in cranberries, nuts, cheese and salt. Sprinkle with parsley.

*For toasted pine nuts, cook over medium heat 5 to 7 minutes, stirring frequently until nuts begin to brown, then stirring constantly until nuts are light brown. Or, bake uncovered 6 to 10 minutes, stirring occasionally until nuts are light brown.

1 Serving: Calories 190 (Calories from Fat 70); Total Fat 8g (Saturated Fat 2g); Cholesterol 5mg; Sodium 340mg; Total Carbohydrate 26g (Dietary Fiber 2g); Protein 5g

Tabbouleh

Prep Time: 10 min ▮ Start to Finish: 1 hr 40 min ▮ 6 servings

¾ cup uncooked bulgur
1½ cups chopped fresh parsley
3 medium tomatoes, chopped (2¼ cups)
5 medium green onions, thinly sliced (⅓ cup)
2 tablespoons chopped fresh or 2 teaspoons crumbled dried mint leaves
¼ cup olive or vegetable oil
¼ cup lemon juice
¾ teaspoon salt
¼ teaspoon pepper
Whole ripe olives, if desired

1 In small bowl, cover bulgur with cold water. Let stand 30 minutes; drain. Press out as much water as possible.

2 In medium glass or plastic bowl, place bulgur, parsley, tomatoes, onions and mint.

3 In tightly-covered container, shake remaining ingredients except olives. Pour over bulgur mixture; toss. Cover and refrigerate at least 1 hour to blend flavors. Garnish with olives.

1 Serving: Calories 160 (Calories from Fat 90); Total Fat 10g (Saturated Fat 1g); Cholesterol 0mg; Sodium 320mg; Total Carbohydrate. 19g (Dietary Fiber 5g); Protein 3g

Southwestern Tabbouleh: Substitute 1 cup chopped fresh cilantro for the parsley. Decrease lemon juice to 2 tablespoons; increase salt to 1 teaspoon. Add 2 teaspoons ground cumin with the remaining ingredients in Step 3.

Tarragon-Couscous Salad

Prep Time: 25 min ▪ Start to Finish: 55 min ▪ 6 servings

3$\frac{1}{3}$ cups water
$\frac{1}{2}$ cup dried red lentils, sorted, rinsed
2 teaspoons olive oil
$\frac{1}{4}$ teaspoon salt
1 cup uncooked whole wheat couscous (from 11-oz box)
3 tablespoons olive oil
3 tablespoons seasoned rice vinegar
1 teaspoon Dijon mustard
1 clove garlic, finely chopped
1 medium carrot, finely chopped ($\frac{1}{2}$ cup)
4 medium green onions, finely chopped ($\frac{1}{4}$ cup)
$\frac{1}{4}$ cup chopped walnuts, toasted*
2 tablespoons chopped fresh parsley
1 tablespoon chopped fresh or 1 teaspoon crushed dried tarragon leaves

1 In 1-quart saucepan, heat 2 cups of the water to boiling. Stir in lentils; reduce heat to low. Cook 10 to 12 minutes or until just tender. Drain; cool 15 minutes.

2 Meanwhile, in 1-quart saucepan, heat remaining 1$\frac{1}{3}$ cups water, 2 teaspoons oil and the salt to boiling. Stir in couscous; remove from heat. Cover; let stand 5 minutes. Fluff couscous lightly with fork. Cool 10 minutes.

3 Meanwhile, in medium bowl, beat 3 tablespoons oil, the vinegar, mustard and garlic with whisk until blended. Stir in carrot, onions, walnuts, parsley and tarragon. Stir in lentils and couscous. Serve immediately or refrigerate until serving.

*For toasted walnuts, cook over medium heat 5 to 7 minutes, stirring frequently until nuts begin to brown, then stirring constantly until nuts are light brown. Or, bake uncovered 6 to 10 minutes, stirring occasionally until nuts are light brown.

1 Serving: Calories 290 (Calories from Fat 110); Total Fat 12g (Saturated Fat 1.5g); Cholesterol 0mg; Sodium 130mg; Total Carbohydrate 35g (Dietary Fiber 6g); Protein 9g

Mediterranean Couscous Salad

Prep Time: 20 min ▪ Start to Finish: 1 hr 20 min ▪ 5 servings

1 cup vegetable or chicken broth (from 32-oz carton)
³/₄ cup uncooked couscous
3 medium plum (Roma) tomatoes, cubed (1 cup)
1 small unpeeled cucumber, cubed (1 cup)
¹/₂ cup halved pitted kalamata olives
4 medium green onions, chopped (¹/₄ cup)
¹/₄ cup chopped fresh or 1 tablespoon dried dill weed
2 tablespoons lemon juice
2 tablespoons olive or vegetable oil
¹/₈ teaspoon salt
2 tablespoons crumbled feta cheese

1 In 2-quart saucepan, heat broth to boiling. Stir in couscous; remove from heat. Cover; let stand 5 minutes.

2 In large bowl, place tomatoes, cucumber, olives, onions and dill weed. Stir in couscous.

3 In small bowl, beat lemon juice, oil and salt with whisk until well blended; pour over vegetable mixture and toss. Cover; refrigerate 1 hour to blend flavors.

4 Just before serving, sprinkle with cheese.

1 Serving: Calories 380 (Calories from Fat 140); Total Fat 16g (Saturated Fat 3g); Cholesterol 5mg; Sodium 790mg; Total Carbohydrate 49g (Dietary Fiber 5g); Protein 10g

What a refreshing and economical dish for a summer party—or, even better, a picnic! Be sure to add the crumbled feta cheese just before serving to preserve its tangy flavor.

3

pasta
salads

Italian Pasta Salad

Prep Time: 30 min ■ Start to Finish: 1 hr ■ 6 servings

Garlic Vinaigrette Dressing

1 clove garlic or $1/8$ teaspoon garlic
    powder
$1/4$ cup cider vinegar or balsamic
    vinegar
2 tablespoons olive or vegetable oil
$1/2$ teaspoon salt

Salad

$1/4$ teaspoon salt (for cooking
    pasta), if desired
2 cups uncooked rotini or rotelle
    (spiral) pasta (6 oz)
1 large tomato
$1/2$ of a medium cucumber
3 or 4 medium green onions
    with tops
1 small red or green bell pepper
$1/4$ cup chopped ripe olives
    (from $4^1/4$-oz can), if desired

1 In tightly-covered jar or container, shake all dressing ingredients.

2 Cook and drain pasta as directed on package. Rinse with cold water; drain.

3 In large bowl, mix pasta and remaining salad ingredients.

4 Shake dressing again to mix ingredients. Pour over vegetables and pasta; mix thoroughly. Cover with plastic wrap; refrigerate about 30 minutes or until chilled.

1 Serving: Calories 230 (Calories from Fat 60); Total Fat 6g (Saturated Fat 1g); Cholesterol 0mg; Sodium 250mg; Total Carbohydrate 37g (Dietary Fiber 3g); Protein 7g

Italian Pepperoni-Pasta Salad: Add one 3.5-oz package sliced pepperoni (cut slices in half) and ½ cup shredded mozzarella or pizza blend cheese.

Ranch Pasta Salad: Use about ½ cup purchased ranch dressing instead of the Garlic Vinaigrette Dressing.

Pesto Macaroni Salad

Prep Time: 5 min ▪ Start to Finish: 2 hr 15 min ▪ 6 servings

3 cups uncooked elbow macaroni (12 oz)
1 tablespoon olive or vegetable oil
1 container (8 oz) pesto
4 plum (Roma) tomatoes, each cut into 4 wedges
1/2 cup small pitted ripe olives
1/4 cup white wine vinegar
4 cups coarsely shredded spinach
Grated Parmesan cheese

1 Cook macaroni as directed on package; drain. Rinse with cold water; drain and toss with oil.

2 In large bowl, mix pesto, tomatoes, olives and vinegar. Arrange 2 cups of the macaroni and 2 cups of the spinach on pesto mixture; repeat with remaining macaroni and spinach.

3 Cover and refrigerate at least 2 hours but no longer than 24 hours. Toss; sprinkle with cheese.

1 Serving: Calories 470 (Calories from Fat 215); Total Fat 24g (Saturated Fat 15g); Cholesterol 150mg; Sodium 220mg; Total Carbohydrate 56g (Dietary Fiber 5g); Protein 13g

Primavera Pasta Salad

Prep Time: 25 min ■ Start to Finish: 25 min ■ 14 servings

3½ cups uncooked bow-tie (farfalle) pasta (9 oz)

2 cups snow pea pods, strings removed (12 oz)

2 large red bell peppers, cut into 1-inch pieces (2 cups)

2 medium carrots, sliced (1 cup)

½ cup chopped fresh basil leaves

½ cup shredded Parmesan cheese (2 oz)

1 cup creamy Parmesan dressing

2 tablespoons milk

1 Cook and drain pasta as directed on package, adding pea pods for last minute of cooking. Rinse with cold water; drain.

2 In very large (4-quart) bowl, mix bell peppers, carrots, basil and cheese. In small bowl, mix dressing and milk with whisk. Add dressing mixture, pasta and pea pods to bell pepper mixture; toss to coat. Serve immediately or store covered in refrigerator until serving time.

1 Serving: Calories 175 (Calories from Fat 80); Total Fat 9g (Saturated Fat 1g); Cholesterol 6mg; Sodium 230mg; Total Carbohydrate 19g (Dietary Fiber 2g); Protein 5g

This colorful salad makes an excellent side dish for grilled chicken, steaks and chops. As a meatless main-dish salad, it can serve up to 6 people.

Vegetable-Pasta Salad

Prep Time: 20 min ▪ Start to Finish: 20 min ▪ 10 servings

Pasta Salad

1 package (16 oz) pasta shells,
   cooked, drained
1½ lb fresh asparagus, cut into
   4-inch pieces
1 lb fresh sugar snap peas, blanched
6 green onions, sliced
1 yellow bell pepper, cut into
   julienne strips

Lemon Mayonnaise

1 cup mayonnaise
½ cup plain yogurt
¼ cup lemon juice
2 tablespoons chopped fresh
   or 2 teaspoons dried
   tarragon leaves
½ teaspoon salt

1 Cook and drain pasta as directed on package. Rinse with cold water; drain.

2 Place asparagus in boiling water. Cover and cook 1 minute; drain. Immediately rinse with cold water; drain.

3 Place snap pea pods in boiling water. Cover and cook 1 minute; drain. Immediately rinse with cold water; drain.

4 Mix all mayonnaise ingredients until well blended.

5 In large bowl, mix pasta, asparagus, snap peas, onions and bell pepper; toss. Stir in mayonnaise until well mixed. Cover and refrigerate until ready to serve.

1 Serving: Calories 365 (Calories from Fat 170); Total Fat 19g (Saturated Fat 3g); Cholesterol 15mg; Sodium 260mg; Total Carbohydrate 43g (Dietary Fiber 4g); Protein 10g

Keep your vegetables fresh and bright by blanching them. It's not hard. Just place vegetables in a wire basket or a blancher, and drop the basket into boiling water. Cover and cook vegetables for about a minute, just until slightly tender. Then remove the basket from the boiling water and immediately plunge the vegetables into iced water to stop cooking.

Greek Pasta Salad

Prep Time: 15 min ▮ Start to Finish: 1 hr 25 min ▮ 5 servings

1¼ cups uncooked orzo or rosamarina pasta (8 oz)
2 cups thinly sliced cucumber (about 2 small)
1 medium red onion, chopped (½ cup)
½ cup Italian dressing
1 medium tomato, chopped (¾ cup)
1 can (15 to 16 oz) garbanzo beans, rinsed and drained
1 can (2¼ oz) sliced ripe olives, drained
½ cup crumbled feta cheese (2 oz)

1 Cook pasta as directed on package; drain. Rinse with cold water; drain.

2 In large glass or plastic bowl, mix pasta and remaining ingredients except cheese. Cover and refrigerate at least 1 hour to blend flavors but no longer than 24 hours.

3 To serve, top salad with cheese.

1 Serving: Calories 445 (Calories from Fat 155); Total Fat 17g (Saturated Fat 3g); Cholesterol 15mg; Sodium 580mg; Total Carbohydrate 66g (Dietary Fiber 9g); Protein 16g

Feta cheese is bursting with sharp, tangy, salty flavor. This crumbly cheese is traditionally made from goat's or sheep's milk, but due to its popularity is often made with cow's milk. Crumbled blue cheese, in place of the feta, is also good on this salad.

Hearty Soybean and Cheddar Pasta Salad

Prep Time: 20 min ▪ Start to Finish: 1 hr 30 min ▪ 6 servings

Dressing

3 tablespoons canola or olive oil

1/4 cup red wine vinegar

1 teaspoon Italian seasoning

1/2 teaspoon salt

1/4 teaspoon pepper

1/4 teaspoon garlic powder

Salad

1 cup uncooked penne pasta (3 oz)

1 box (10 oz) frozen soybeans
(about 2 cups)

2 large tomatoes, coarsely chopped
(2 cups)

1 medium cucumber, coarsely
chopped (1 cup)

2 small yellow bell peppers,
coarsely chopped (1 cup)

3 oz Cheddar cheese, cut into 1/2-
inch cubes (3/4 cup)

1 In small bowl, beat all dressing ingredients with whisk until well mixed.

2 Cook and drain pasta as directed on package. Rinse with cold water; drain.

3 Meanwhile, cook soybeans as directed on package. Rinse with cold water; drain.

4 In large bowl, toss pasta, soybeans, remaining salad ingredients and dressing. Cover and refrigerate at least 1 hour before serving.

1 Serving: Calories 270 (Calories from Fat 130); Total Fat 15g (Saturated Fat 4g); Cholesterol 15mg; Sodium 350mg; Total Carbohydrate 22g (Dietary Fiber 4g); Protein 12g

Frozen green soybeans (also called edamame) are a handy and healthy snack on their own, very high in protein and fiber, and quite inexpensive. They're sold in and out of their pods. For this recipe, you'd want them out of the pod. They're used as a tasty centerpiece in this cheesy veggie pasta salad.

Lemon-Basil Chicken-Pasta Salad

Prep Time: 25 min ■ Start to Finish: 1 hr 25 min ■ 4 servings

$\frac{1}{2}$ teaspoon salt (for cooking pasta), if desired

2 cups uncooked rotini or rotelle pasta (6 oz)

10 asparagus stalks (about 8 oz)

5 oz cooked chicken or turkey

1 clove garlic or $\frac{1}{8}$ teaspoon garlic powder

$\frac{1}{2}$ cup fresh basil leaves

$\frac{1}{2}$ cup shredded Parmesan cheese (2 oz)

$\frac{1}{4}$ cup olive or vegetable oil

1 tablespoon grated lemon peel

1 Cook and drain pasta as directed on package, adding asparagus during last 2 to 3 minutes of cooking.

2 In large glass or plastic bowl, toss pasta, asparagus and chicken. Stir in garlic, basil, cheese, oil and lemon peel. Cover with plastic wrap; refrigerate 1 to 2 hours or until chilled.

1 Serving: Calories 440 (Calories from Fat 190); Total Fat 21g; Cholesterol 45mg; Sodium 250mg; Total Carbohydrate 39g (Dietary Fiber 3g); Protein 24g

Chicken and Tortellini Salad

Prep Time: 20 min ▪ Start to Finish: 2 hr 20 min ▪ 4 servings

1 package (7 oz) dried cheese-filled tortellini

$1/3$ cup chicken broth

1 tablespoon chopped fresh or 1 teaspoon dried tarragon leaves

2 tablespoons olive or vegetable oil

2 tablespoons lemon juice

1 teaspoon sugar

$1/2$ teaspoon salt

$1/4$ teaspoon pepper

$1 1/2$ cups cut-up cooked chicken or turkey

3 cups bite-size pieces mixed greens

1 small bell pepper (any color), cut into $1/2$-inch squares

1 Cook pasta as directed on package. Meanwhile, in tightly-covered container, shake chicken broth, tarragon, oil, lemon juice, sugar, salt and pepper until well mixed. Drain pasta; rinse with cold water. In large bowl, combine pasta and chicken. Add dressing and toss to coat. Cover and refrigerate at least 2 hours or overnight.

2 Just before serving, add greens and bell pepper to pasta mixture; toss to combine.

1 Serving: Calories 300 (Calories from Fat 120); Total Fat 14g (Saturated Fat 3.5g); Cholesterol 70mg; Sodium 730mg; Total Carbohydrate 23g (Dietary Fiber 1g); Protein 21g

Chicken-Pasta Salad with Pesto

Prep Time: 10 min ■ Start to Finish: 25 min ■ 4 servings

6 oz uncooked multicolored bow-tie (farfalle) pasta (about 2¹/₄ cups)
1¹/₂ cups cut-up cooked chicken
¹/₄ cup sun-dried tomatoes in oil, drained, chopped
1 medium bell pepper, cut into strips
1 small zucchini, thinly sliced
¹/₂ small red onion, sliced
¹/₃ cup basil pesto

1 Cook pasta as directed on package; drain. Rinse with cold water; drain.

2 In large bowl, mix pasta, chicken, tomatoes, bell pepper, zucchini and onion. Stir in pesto.

1 Serving: Calories 405 (Calories from Fat 155); Total Fat 17g (Saturated Fat 4g); Cholesterol 50mg; Sodium 250mg; Total Carbohydrate 40g (Dietary Fiber 3g); Protein 23g

Pasta is pretty interchangeable, as long as you stay with similar sizes. Try using radiatore, mafalda or rotelle pasta instead of the farfalle in this recipe.

Pasta Salad with Salmon and Dill

Prep Time: 10 min ■ Start to Finish: 20 min ■ 4 servings

8 oz uncooked fettuccine
2 medium carrots
2 medium zucchini
1 can (7.5 oz) boneless, skinless red sockeye salmon, drained and flaked
1 container (8 oz) refrigerated dill dip
$^3/_4$ teaspoon lemon pepper

1 Cook and drain fettuccine as directed on package. Rinse with cold water; drain.

2 Cut carrots and zucchini lengthwise into thin slices, using vegetable peeler.

3 In large bowl, toss fettucine, vegetables and remaining ingredients. Serve immediately or refrigerate 1 to 2 hours or until chilled.

1 Serving: Calories 390 (Calories from Fat 135); Total Fat 15g (Saturated Fat 7g); Cholesterol 95mg; Sodium 760mg; Total Carbohydrate 46g (Dietary Fiber 3g); Protein 20g

Tuna-Macaroni Salad

Prep Time: 20 min ▪ Start to Finish: 1 hr 20 min ▪ 6 servings

1 package (7 oz) elbow macaroni
$1/2$ cup frozen green peas
1 can (9 oz) tuna, drained
1 cup mayonnaise or salad dressing
1 cup shredded Cheddar cheese (4 oz), if desired
$1/4$ cup sweet pickle relish, if desired
2 teaspoons lemon juice
$3/4$ teaspoon salt
$1/4$ teaspoon pepper
1 medium stalk celery, chopped ($1/2$ cup)
1 small onion, chopped ($1/4$ cup)

1 Cook macaroni as directed on package, adding peas for last 4 to 6 minutes of cooking. Rinse with cold water; drain.

2 In large bowl, mix macaroni, peas and remaining ingredients. Cover and refrigerate at least 1 hour to blend flavors.

1 Serving (about 1 cup): Calories 450 (Calories from Fat 270); Total Fat 30g (Saturated Fat 5g); Cholesterol 35mg; Sodium 660mg; Total Carbohydrate 30g (Dietary Fiber 2g); Protein 16g

Lighter Tuna-Macaroni Salad: For 1 gram of fat and 210 calories per serving, use fat-free mayonnaise, reduced-fat Cheddar cheese and water-packed tuna.

Shrimp-Pasta Salad Toss

Prep Time: 10 min ▪ Start to Finish: 10 min ▪ 2 servings

6 oz cooked deveined peeled shrimp, thawed if frozen,
   tail shells removed
2 cups bite-size pieces spinach
1/2 pint deli pasta salad (1 cup)
1/2 cup cherry tomatoes, cut in half
2 tablespoons sliced ripe olives

In large bowl, toss all ingredients.

1 Serving: Calories 300 (Calories from Fat 115); Total Fat 13g (Saturated Fat 2g); Cholesterol 175mg; Sodium 630mg; Total Carbohydrate 26g (Dietary Fiber 3g); Protein 23g

If your favorite deli pasta salad is too thick for this recipe, thin it by stirring in a tablespoon of milk until you get the consistency you like. This recipe is perfect to double, or even triple, if you want to serve more people.

Shrimp Pasta Salad with Fresh Fruit Salsa

Prep Time: 30 min ■ Start to Finish: 30 min ■ 6 servings

Pasta Salad

2 cups uncooked bow-tie (farfalle) pasta (4 oz)

1 head Boston lettuce, separated into leaves

1 medium cucumber, cut lengthwise in half, then sliced crosswise

18 cooked large (21 to 30 count) deveined peeled shrimp with
 tail shells left on (about ³/₄ lb)

1 large avocado, pitted, peeled and sliced

Fresh Fruit Salsa

¹/₂ cup coarsely chopped pineapple

¹/₂ cup coarsely chopped strawberries

2 kiwifruit, peeled, coarsely chopped

1 small jalapeño chile, chopped

2 tablespoons orange juice

1 tablespoon olive or vegetable oil

1 teaspoon grated orange peel

¹/₄ teaspoon salt

¹/₈ teaspoon white pepper

1 Cook pasta as directed on package. Meanwhile, divide lettuce among 6 serving plates. Arrange cucumber, shrimp and avocado on plates.

2 In small bowl, mix salsa ingredients. Drain pasta and rinse in cold water; divide among salads. Serve with salsa.

1 Serving: Calories 230 (Calories from Fat 70); Total Fat 8g (Saturated Fat 1g); Cholesterol 125mg; Sodium 230mg; Total Carbohydrate 24g (Dietary Fiber 4g); Protein 15g

Lo Mein Noodle Salad

Prep Time: 20 min ▪ Start to Finish: 20 min ▪ 6 servings

Salad

1 package (8 oz) lo mein noodles

1 bag (10 oz) frozen shelled edamame (green) soybeans

1 large red bell pepper, chopped (1½ cups)

4 medium green onions, sliced (¼ cup)

Dressing

⅓ cup rice vinegar

⅓ cup peanut butter

¼ cup soy sauce

2 tablespoons packed brown sugar

2 tablespoons vegetable oil

¼ teaspoon crushed red pepper flakes

1 Break lo mein noodles into thirds. Cook as directed on package. Rinse with cold water; drain.

2 Cook edamame as directed on bag; drain.

3 In medium bowl, place bell pepper, onions, noodles and edamame.

4 In small bowl, beat dressing ingredients with whisk until well blended. Spoon over noodle mixture; toss to coat. Serve immediately, or cover and refrigerate until serving time.

1 Serving: Calories 400 (Calories from Fat 140); Total Fat 15g (Saturated Fat 2.5g); Cholesterol 0mg; Sodium 820mg; Total Carbohydrate 48g (Dietary Fiber 6g); Protein 16g

Here's a fun use for the peanut butter in your pantry—a cold noodle salad that's healthy and not at all costly. It's a great dish to serve either at room temperature or chilled.

Noodles and Peanut Sauce Salad Bowl

Prep Time: 25 min ▪ Start to Finish: 25 min ▪ 4 servings

8 oz uncooked whole wheat linguine, broken in half

2 cups fresh broccoli florets

1 cup julienne carrots (from 10-oz bag)

1 medium bell pepper, cut into bite-size pieces

$1/4$ cup peanut butter

2 tablespoons water

2 teaspoons canola oil

2 tablespoons rice vinegar or white vinegar

2 tablespoons reduced-sodium soy sauce

$1/2$ teaspoon ground ginger

$1/8$ teaspoon ground red pepper (cayenne)

3 medium green onions, chopped (3 tablespoons)

3 tablespoons chopped fresh cilantro

1 Cook pasta as directed on package, adding broccoli, carrots and bell pepper during last minute of cooking; drain pasta and vegetables. Rinse with cold water until pasta and vegetables are cool; drain.

2 In small bowl, place peanut butter. Gradually beat water and oil into peanut butter with whisk until smooth. Beat in vinegar, soy sauce, ginger and ground red pepper until blended.

3 In large serving bowl, stir together pasta mixture, peanut sauce, onions and cilantro until well mixed.

1 Serving (1³/₄ cups each): Calories 370 (Calories from Fat 100); Total Fat 12g (Saturated Fat 2g); Cholesterol 0mg; Sodium 570mg; Total Carbohydrate 51g (Dietary Fiber 8g); Protein 14g

Grilled Chicken Citrus Salad

Gingered Chicken and Fruit Salad

Crunchy Oriental Chicken Salad

Chicken-Grapefruit Salad

Tarragon Chicken Salad

Summer Harvest Chicken-Potato Salad

Wild Rice–Chicken Salad

Italian Chopped Salad

Southwestern Chicken BLT Salad

Sausalito Chicken and Seafood Salad

Cobb Salad

Turkey Taco Salad

Curried Turkey Salad

Southwestern Turkey Salad

Turkey Salad with Fruit

Turkey and Dried Cherry Salad

Grilled Balsamic-Beef Salad

Fajita Salad

Grilled Steak and Potato Salad

Fiesta Taco Salad

Asian Pork Salad

Bacon-Spinach Salad

Ten-Minute Ham Salad

Italian Ham and Pasta Salad

1

poultry, beef and pork salads

Grilled Chicken Citrus Salad

Prep Time: 30 min ▪ Start to Finish: 30 min ▪ 4 servings

$^2/_3$ cup citrus vinaigrette dressing

4 boneless skinless chicken breasts (about 1$^1/_4$ lb)

1 bag (10 oz) ready-to-eat romaine lettuce

2 unpeeled apples, cubed (about 2 cups)

$^1/_2$ cup coarsely chopped dried apricots

2 medium green onions, sliced (2 tablespoons)

$^1/_2$ cup chopped honey-roasted peanuts

1 Heat gas or charcoal grill. In small bowl, place 2 tablespoons of the dressing. Brush all sides of chicken with the 2 tablespoons dressing.

2 In large bowl, toss lettuce, apples, apricots and onions; set aside.

3 Place chicken on grill. Cover grill; cook over medium heat 8 to 10 minutes, turning once, until juice of chicken is clear when center of thickest part is cut (170°F).

4 Add remaining dressing to lettuce mixture; toss. On 4 plates, divide lettuce mixture. Cut chicken crosswise into slices; place on lettuce. Sprinkle with peanuts.

1 Serving: Calories 550 (Calories from Fat 280); Total Fat 31g (Saturated Fat 4g); Cholesterol 90mg; Sodium 510mg; Total Carbohydrate 30g (Dietary Fiber 6g); Protein 39g

Gingered Chicken and Fruit Salad

Prep Time: 25 min ‖ Start to Finish: 25 min ‖ 4 servings

Ginger Dressing
1/2 teaspoon grated lime peel
2 tablespoons fresh lime juice
2 tablespoons canola oil
1 tablespoon water
2 teaspoons honey
1/2 teaspoon ground ginger

Salad
6 cups fresh baby spinach leaves
2 cups cubed cooked chicken breast
1 ripe medium mango, seed removed, peeled and cubed
1 cup seedless red grapes, cut in half
2 medium green onions, sliced (2 tablespoons)
2 tablespoons coarsely chopped pecans, toasted*

1 In tightly-covered container, shake dressing ingredients until well mixed.

2 Divide spinach among 4 serving plates. Top each with chicken, mango, grapes, onions and pecans. Drizzle with dressing.

*For toasted pecans, cook over medium heat 5 to 7 minutes, stirring frequently until nuts begin to brown, then stirring constantly until nuts are light brown. Or, bake uncovered 6 to 10 minutes, stirring occasionally until nuts are light brown.

1 Serving: Calories 290 (Calories from Fat 110); Total Fat 13g (Saturated Fat 1.5g); Cholesterol 55mg; Sodium 90mg; Total Carbohydrate 22g (Dietary Fiber 3g); Protein 23g

Crunchy Oriental Chicken Salad

Prep Time: 10 min ▌ Start to Finish: 15 min ▌ 6 servings

2 tablespoons butter or margarine
1 package (3 oz) Oriental-flavor ramen noodle soup mix
2 tablespoons sesame seed
$\frac{1}{4}$ cup sugar
$\frac{1}{4}$ cup white vinegar
1 tablespoon sesame or vegetable oil
$\frac{1}{2}$ teaspoon pepper
2 cups cut-up cooked chicken
$\frac{1}{4}$ cup dry-roasted peanuts, if desired
4 medium green onions, sliced ($\frac{1}{4}$ cup)
1 bag (16 oz) coleslaw mix
1 can (11 oz) mandarin orange segments, drained

1 In 10-inch skillet, melt butter over medium heat. Stir in seasoning packet from soup mix. Break block of noodles into bite-size pieces over skillet; stir into butter mixture.

2 Cook noodles 2 minutes, stirring occasionally. Stir in sesame seed. Cook about 2 minutes longer, stirring occasionally, until noodles are golden brown; remove from heat.

3 In large glass or plastic bowl, mix sugar, vinegar, oil and pepper. Add noodle mixture and remaining ingredients; toss. Serve immediately.

1 Serving: Calories. 265 (Calories from Fat 110); Total Fat 12g (Saturated Fat 4g); Cholesterol 50mg; Sodium 260mg; Total Carbohydrates 25g (Dietary Fiber 2g); Protein 16g

Chicken-Grapefruit Salad

Prep Time: 15 min ▌ Start to Finish: 1 hr 15 min ▌ 6 servings

Dressing
$^2/_3$ cup plain fat-free yogurt
$^1/_2$ cup finely chopped peeled cucumber
3 tablespoons grapefruit juice
2 tablespoons light mayonnaise or salad dressing
1 teaspoon prepared horseradish
$^1/_4$ teaspoon pepper

Salad
3 cups cubed cooked chicken
2 cups red grapefruit sections (2 large grapefruit)
$^3/_4$ cup chopped peeled cucumber
1 medium avocado, peeled, pitted, and coarsely chopped
5 cups watercress sprigs (2 large bunches) or arugula

1 In large bowl, mix dressing ingredients with whisk or spoon. Add chicken, grapefruit, cucumber and avocado; gently toss until evenly coated.

2 Cover and refrigerate about 1 hour or until chilled. Arrange watercress on 6 plates; top with salad.

1 Serving: Calories 230 (Calories from Fat 70); Total Fat 7g (Saturated Fat 1.5g); Cholesterol 60mg; Sodium 150mg; Total Carbohydrate 16g (Dietary Fiber 3g); Protein 25g

Tarragon Chicken Salad

Prep Time: 10 min ▪ Start to Finish: 15 min ▪ 4 servings

$^1/_2$ cup mayonnaise
$^1/_2$ cup plain yogurt
2 tablespoons tarragon vinegar
1 tablespoon chopped fresh or 1 teaspoon dried tarragon leaves
4 cups cut-up cooked chicken
1 cup chopped pecans, toasted*
2 cups honeydew balls
Lettuce
Melon slices

1 In large bowl, mix mayonnaise, yogurt, vinegar and tarragon. Toss with chicken, pecans and honeydew balls.

2 Arrange lettuce on 4 plates; top with salad and serve with slices of melon.

*For toasted, cook over medium heat 5 to 7 minutes, stirring frequently until nuts begin to brown, then stirring constantly until nuts are light brown. Or, bake uncovered 6 to 10 minutes, stirring occasionally until nuts are light brown.

1 Serving: Calories 710 (Calories from Fat 475); Total Fat 53g (Saturated Fat 8g); Cholesterol 140mg; Sodium 300mg; Total Carbohydrate 17g (Dietary Fiber 3g); Protein 44g

Summer Harvest Chicken-Potato Salad

Prep Time: 15 min ▮ Start to Finish: 30 min ▮ 4 servings

4 medium red potatoes (1 lb), cut into ³/₄-inch cubes

¹/₂ lb fresh green beans, trimmed, cut into 1-inch pieces (about 2 cups)

¹/₂ cup plain fat-free yogurt

¹/₃ cup fat-free ranch dressing

1 tablespoon prepared horseradish

¹/₄ teaspoon salt

Dash pepper

2 cups cut-up cooked chicken breast

²/₃ cup thinly sliced celery

Torn salad greens, if desired

1 In 2-quart saucepan, heat 6 cups lightly salted water to boiling. Add potatoes; return to boiling. Reduce heat; simmer uncovered 5 minutes. Add green beans; cook uncovered 8 to 12 minutes longer or until potatoes and beans are crisp-tender.

2 Meanwhile, in small bowl, mix yogurt, dressing, horseradish, salt and pepper; set aside.

3 Drain potatoes and green beans; rinse with cold water to cool. In large serving bowl, mix potatoes, green beans, chicken and celery. Pour yogurt mixture over salad; toss gently to coat. Line 4 plates with greens; spoon salad onto greens.

1 Serving: Calories 270 (Calories from Fat 35); Total Fat 3.5g (Saturated Fat 1g); Cholesterol 60mg; Sodium 410mg; Total Carbohydrate 32g (Dietary Fiber 5g); Protein 6g

Can't decide between chicken or potato salad? Here you get the best of both! This summery salad keeps the calories down by using fat-free yogurt and ranch dressing, but you can use regular if that's what you have on hand. You could also substitute 2 cups of chopped cooked ham for the chicken.

Wild Rice–Chicken Salad

Prep Time: 15 min ▪ Start to Finish: 15 min ▪ 4 servings

Basil Vinaigrette
$1/4$ cup olive or vegetable oil

3 tablespoons raspberry vinegar or red wine vinegar

1 tablespoon chopped fresh basil leaves

$1/4$ teaspoon salt

$1/4$ teaspoon pepper

Salad
1 pint (2 cups) deli chicken salad

1 can (15 oz) cooked wild rice, drained

$1/2$ cup dried cranberries

Boston lettuce leaves

1 In small bowl, mix all vinaigrette ingredients.

2 In large bowl, mix all salad ingredients except lettuce. Toss with vinaigrette until coated. Arrange lettuce on 4 plates; top with salad.

1 Serving: Calories 475 (Calories from Fat 235); Total Fat 26g (Saturated Fat 4g); Cholesterol 45mg; Sodium 380mg; Total Carbohydrate 42g (Dietary Fiber 4g); Protein 18g

Italian Chopped Salad

Prep Time: 25 min ▪ Start to Finish: 25 min ▪ 4 servings

6 cups chopped (1 large bunch or 2 small bunches) romaine lettuce
2 large tomatoes, chopped (2 cups)
2 medium cucumbers, chopped (1½ cups)
1 cup cut-up cooked chicken or turkey
1 package (3 oz) Italian salami, chopped
1 can (15 to 16 oz) cannellini beans, rinsed, drained
1 cup fresh basil leaves
⅔ cup red wine vinaigrette or Italian dressing

In large bowl, place all ingredients except vinaigrette. Pour vinaigrette over salad; toss until coated.

1 Serving: Calories 500 (Calories from Fat 260); Total Fat 29g (Saturated Fat 6g); Cholesterol 55mg; Sodium 1050mg; Total Carbohydrate 33g (Dietary Fiber 9g); Protein 27g

Southwestern Chicken BLT Salad

Prep Time: 20 min ▪ Start to Finish: 20 min ▪ 6 servings

Salsa-Bacon Dressing
$1/2$ cup chunky-style salsa
$1/2$ cup nonfat ranch dressing
1 tablespoon chopped fresh parsley

Salad
1 bag (10 oz) romaine and leaf lettuce mix
2 packages (6 oz each) refrigerated cooked
    Southwest-flavor chicken breast strips
4 plum (Roma) tomatoes, coarsely chopped
$1/2$ cup chopped cooked bacon
$1/2$ cup croutons

1 In small bowl, mix all dressing ingredients; set aside.

2 In large bowl, mix remaining ingredients. Add dressing; toss until coated.

1 Serving: Calories 190 (Calories from Fat 60); Total Fat 7g (Saturated Fat 2g); Cholesterol 55mg; Sodium 530mg; Total Carbohydrate 12g (Dietary Fiber 2g); Protein 21g

Sausalito Chicken and Seafood Salad

Prep Time: 20 min ▌ Start to Finish: 20 min ▌ 4 servings

6 cups bite-size pieces assorted salad greens

1 cup diced rotisserie or other cooked chicken

1 large avocado, pitted, peeled and sliced

1 package (8 oz) refrigerated chunk-style imitation crabmeat

1 can (4 oz) whole green chiles, drained, sliced lengthwise

3/4 cup frozen (thawed) guacamole (from 12-oz container)

1/2 cup sour cream

1 large tomato, chopped (1 cup)

Lime or lemon wedges

1 Among 4 plates, divide salad greens. Top with chicken, avocado, crabmeat and chiles.

2 In small bowl, mix guacamole and sour cream; spoon over salad. Top with tomato. Garnish with lime wedges.

1 Serving: Calories 360 (Calories from Fat 190); Total Fat 21g (Saturated Fat 6g); Cholesterol 65mg; Sodium 1400mg; Total Carbohydrate 20g (Dietary Fiber 9g); Protein 23g

Cobb Salad

Prep Time: 10 min ▮ Start to Finish: 1 hr 10 min ▮ 4 servings

Lemon Vinaigrette
1/2 cup vegetable oil
1/4 cup lemon juice
1 tablespoon red wine vinegar
2 teaspoons sugar
1/2 teaspoon salt
1/2 teaspoon ground mustard
1/2 teaspoon Worcestershire sauce
1/4 teaspoon pepper
1 clove garlic, finely chopped

Salad
1 small head lettuce, finely
   shredded (6 cups)
2 cups cut-up cooked chicken
3 hard-cooked eggs, chopped
2 medium tomatoes, chopped
   (1 1/2 cups)
1 medium ripe avocado, pitted,
   peeled and chopped
1/4 cup crumbled blue cheese (1 oz)
4 slices bacon, crisply cooked,
   crumbled (1/4 cup)

1 In tightly-covered container, shake all vinaigrette ingredients. Refrigerate at least 1 hour to blend flavors.

2 Divide lettuce among 4 salad plates or shallow bowls. Arrange remaining salad ingredients in rows on lettuce. Serve with vinaigrette.

1 Serving: Calories 590 (Calories from Fat 440); Total Fat 49g (Saturated Fat 10g); Cholesterol 230mg; Sodium 630mg; Total Carbohydrate 12g (Dietary Fiber 4g); Protein 30g

Turkey Taco Salad

Prep Time: 10 min ▪ Start to Finish: 20 min ▪ 4 servings

1 lb ground turkey
3/4 cup water
2 teaspoons chili powder
1/2 teaspoon salt
1/2 teaspoon ground cumin
1 small onion, finely chopped (1/4 cup)
1 clove garlic, finely chopped
1 can (11 oz) whole kernel corn, drained
6 cups corn tortilla chips (3 oz)
4 cups shredded iceberg lettuce
1 medium tomato, chopped (3/4 cup)
1 cup chunky-style salsa

1 In 10-inch skillet, cook turkey, water, chili powder, salt, cumin, onion and garlic over medium-high heat 10 to 12 minutes, stirring frequently, until turkey is no longer pink and liquid is absorbed. Stir in corn. Cover and keep warm over low heat.

2 Arrange tortilla chips on large serving plate. Top with lettuce, tomato, turkey mixture and salsa.

1 Serving: Calories 395 (Calories from Fat 160); Total Fat 18g (Saturated Fat 4g); Cholesterol 75mg; Sodium 1,160mg; Total Carbohydrate 35g (Dietary Fiber 5g); Protein 28g

What a great salad to serve at your next fiesta! For beef lovers, use lean ground beef instead of the turkey. Have colorful bowls of additional toppings, such as sliced black olives, sour cream and sliced jalapeño peppers—for those who like it "hot."

Curried Turkey Salad

Prep Time: 5 min ▮ Start to Finish: 2 hr 20 min ▮ 6 servings

1½ cups uncooked elbow macaroni (6 oz)
1 package (10 oz) frozen green peas
³/₄ cup mayonnaise or salad dressing
2 teaspoons curry powder
2 cups cut-up cooked turkey breast
½ cup shredded Cheddar cheese (2 oz)
4 medium green onions, sliced (¼ cup)
1 medium stalk celery, sliced (½ cup)
Lettuce leaves, if desired

1 Cook and drain macaroni as directed on package. Rinse with cold water; drain. Rinse frozen peas with cold water to separate; drain.

2 In large bowl, mix mayonnaise and curry powder. Stir in macaroni, peas and remaining ingredients except lettuce. Cover and refrigerate 2 to 4 hours to blend flavors. Serve on lettuce.

1 Serving: Calories 465 (Calories from Fat 250); Total Fat 28g (Saturated Fat 6g); Cholesterol 60mg; Sodium 290mg; Total Carbohydrate 34g (Dietary Fiber 4g); Protein 23g

Did you know curry isn't just one spice? It's a mixture of up to 20 different spices, including cardamom, nutmeg, cinnamon, cloves, coriander and black pepper. In India, people grind fresh curry powder daily. The flavor of those curries can vary dramatically from region to region.

Southwestern Turkey Salad

Prep Time: 15 min ▌ Start to Finish: 30 min ▌ 4 servings

$3/4$ lb ground turkey breast

$1/4$ teaspoon garlic powder

2 tablespoons all-purpose flour

1 can (15 oz) chili beans, undrained

1 tablespoon ground cumin

$1\frac{1}{2}$ teaspoons chili powder

$1/2$ teaspoon onion salt

$1/8$ teaspoon pepper

6 cups bite-size pieces iceberg
    lettuce

1 medium onion, chopped ($1/2$ cup)

1 medium green bell pepper,
    chopped (1 cup)

2 medium tomatoes, chopped
    ($1\frac{1}{2}$ cups)

$1/2$ cup shredded reduced-fat
    Cheddar cheese (4 oz)

$2/3$ cup salsa

$1/3$ cup reduced-calorie Catalina
    dressing

1 cup fat-free sour cream

1 In 10-inch nonstick skillet, cook turkey over medium heat, stirring occasionally, until no longer pink. (If turkey sticks to skillet, add up to 2 tablespoons water.) Stir in garlic powder, flour, beans, cumin, chili powder, onion salt and pepper. Cook about 5 minutes or until thickened and bubbly.

2 Divide lettuce among 4 plates. Top with turkey mixture, onion, bell pepper, tomatoes and cheese. In small bowl, mix salsa and dressing; serve with salad. Top salad with sour cream.

1 Serving: Calories 240 (Calories from Fat 125); Total Fat 14g (Saturated Fat 6g); Cholesterol 70mg; Sodium 350mg; Total Carbohydrate 9g (Dietary Fiber 3g); Protein 23g

This turkey salad also makes a great filling for hard or soft tacos, or you can serve it over tortilla chips.

Turkey Salad with Fruit

Prep Time: 20 min   Start to Finish: 2 hr 20 min   4 servings

1 container (6 oz) peach, orange or lemon yogurt ($^2/_3$ cup)
$^1/_4$ teaspoon ground ginger
10 oz cooked turkey or chicken, cut into $^1/_2$-inch pieces (2 cups)
2 medium stalks celery, thinly sliced (1 cup)
1 medium green onion with top, cut into $^1/_8$-inch slices
1 can (11 oz) mandarin orange segments, drained
1 can (8 oz) sliced water chestnuts, drained
1 cup seedless green grapes
4 cups mixed salad greens

1 In large bowl, mix yogurt and ginger. Stir in remaining ingredients except salad greens. Cover with plastic wrap; refrigerate at least 2 hours.

2 On 4 plates, arrange salad greens. Top greens with turkey salad.

1 Serving: Calories 270 (Calories from Fat 50); Total Fat 6g (Saturated Fat 2g); Cholesterol 65mg; Sodium 135mg; Total Carbohydrate 29g (Dietary Fiber 4g); Protein 25g

Containers of fruit yogurt make great snacks—and here you use one to make a simple dressing for this turkey and fruit salad. Use whichever flavor you like best!

Turkey and Dried Cherry Salad

Prep Time 20 min ▮ Start to Finish: 30 min ▮ 4 servings

> 2 cups uncooked gemelli pasta (8 oz)
> 1¹/₂ cups cubed cooked turkey
> ¹/₂ cup dried cherries
> ¹/₄ cup slivered almonds, toasted*
> 1 medium stalk celery, thinly sliced (¹/₂ cup)
> 3 or 4 medium green onions, chopped (about ¹/₄ cup)
> ³/₄ cup refrigerated poppy seed dressing

1 Cook and drain pasta as directed on package.

2 In large bowl, mix pasta and remaining ingredients except dressing. Pour dressing over mixture; toss until coated. Serve immediately, or cover and refrigerate until serving.

*For toasted almonds, cook over medium heat 5 to 7 minutes, stirring frequently until nuts begin to brown, then stirring constantly until nuts are light brown. Or, bake uncovered 6 to 10 minutes, stirring occasionally until nuts are light brown.

1 Serving: Calories 650 (Calories from Fat 270); Total Fat 30g (Saturated Fat 5g); Cholesterol 45mg; Sodium 60mg; Total Carbohydrate 70g (Dietary Fiber 4g); Protein 24g

Grilled Balsamic-Beef Salad

Prep Time: 35 min ▮ Start to Finish: 2 hr 35 min ▮ 6 servings

Balsamic Vinaigrette

$1/2$ cup balsamic vinegar

$1/4$ cup water

1 package Italian dressing mix

1 tablespoon olive oil

Salad

1 boneless beef sirloin steak, 1 to $1^1/2$ inches thick (1 lb)

4 cups fresh baby salad greens

2 cups bite-size pieces arugula leaves

2 plum (Roma) tomatoes, chopped

$1^1/2$ cups sliced baby portabella mushrooms (4 oz)

$3/4$ cup shredded reduced-fat mozzarella cheese (3 oz)

$2/3$ cup Caesar-flavored croutons

1 In tightly-covered container, shake vinaigrette ingredients until well mixed. Divide dressing mixture in half.

2 Place beef in shallow glass or plastic dish or heavy-duty resealable food-storage plastic bag. Pour half of the vinaigrette mixture over beef; turn beef to coat. Cover dish or seal bag; refrigerate at least 2 hours to marinate. Cover; refrigerate remaining vinaigrette.

3 Heat gas or charcoal grill. Remove beef from marinade; reserve marinade. Place beef on grill. Cover grill; cook over medium heat 15 to 20 minutes, turning and brushing with marinade occasionally, until desired doneness. Discard any remaining marinade. Cut beef into 3 × ¼-inch slices.

4 Among 6 plates, divide salad greens, arugula, tomatoes and mushrooms. Top with beef; drizzle with remaining vinaigrette. Sprinkle with cheese and croutons.

1 Serving: Calories 200 (Calories from Fat 80); Total Fat 9g (Saturated Fat 3g); Cholesterol 50mg; Sodium 590mg; Total Carbohydrate 9g (Dietary Fiber 2g); Protein 23g

Fajita Salad

Prep Time: 20 min ▮ Start to Finish: 20 min ▮ 4 servings

¾ lb lean boneless beef sirloin steak

1 tablespoon vegetable oil

2 medium bell peppers, cut into strips

1 small onion, thinly sliced

4 cups bite-size pieces salad greens

⅓ cup Italian dressing

¼ cup plain yogurt

1 Cut beef with grain into 2-inch strips; cut strips across grain into ⅛-inch slices.

2 In 10-inch nonstick skillet, heat oil over medium-high heat. Cook beef in oil about 3 minutes, stirring occasionally, until brown. Remove beef from skillet.

3 Cook bell peppers and onion in same skillet about 3 minutes, stirring occasionally, until bell peppers are crisp-tender. Stir in beef.

4 Place salad greens on serving platter. Top with beef mixture. In small bowl, mix dressing and yogurt; drizzle over salad.

1 Serving: Calories 255 (Calories from Fat 135); Total Fat 15g (Saturated Fat 2g); Cholesterol 50mg; Sodium 240mg; Total Carbohydrate 10g (Dietary Fiber 3g); Protein 20g

Check out the meat case for precut meats. In addition to being a time-saver, these precut meats often come in small, one-time-use portions, which increase your options.

Grilled Steak and Potato Salad

Prep Time: 30 min ▮ Start to Finish: 30 min ▮ 4 servings

³/₄ lb small red potatoes, cut in half

²/₃ cup honey Dijon dressing

1 boneless beef top sirloin or round steak, ³/₄ inch thick (³/₄ lb)

¹/₄ teaspoon salt

¹/₄ teaspoon coarsely ground pepper

4 cups bite-size pieces romaine lettuce

2 medium tomatoes, cut into thin wedges

¹/₂ cup thinly sliced red onion

1 Heat gas or charcoal grill. In 2- or 2½-quart saucepan, place potatoes; add enough water to cover potatoes. Heat to boiling; reduce heat to medium. Cook uncovered 5 to 8 minutes or just until potatoes are tender.

2 Drain potatoes; place in medium bowl. Add 2 tablespoons of the dressing; toss to coat. Place potatoes in grill basket (grill "wok") if desired. Brush beef steak with 1 tablespoon of the dressing; sprinkle with salt and pepper.

3 Place beef and potatoes on grill. Cover grill; cook over medium heat 8 to 15 minutes, turning once, until beef is desired doneness and potatoes are golden brown. Cut beef into thin slices.

4 Among 4 plates, divide lettuce, tomatoes and onion. Top with beef and potatoes; drizzle with remaining dressing. Sprinkle with additional pepper if desired.

1 Serving: Calories 360 (Calories from Fat 180); Total Fat 20g (Saturated Fat 4g); Cholesterol 35mg; Sodium 440mg; Total Carbohydrate 25g (Dietary Fiber 4g); Protein 22g

Try adding a generous sprinkle of crumbled blue or Gorgonzola cheese to top these salads.

Fiesta Taco Salad

Prep Time: 25 min ▪ Start to Finish: 25 min ▪ 5 servings

1 lb lean (at least 80%) ground beef
$^1/_2$ cup taco sauce
6 cups bite-size pieces lettuce
1 medium green bell pepper, cut into strips
2 medium tomatoes, cut into wedges
$^1/_2$ cup pitted ripe olives, drained
1 cup corn chips
1 cup shredded Cheddar cheese (4 oz)
$^1/_2$ cup Thousand Island dressing

1 In 10-inch skillet, cook beef over medium heat 8 to 10 minutes, stirring occasionally, until brown; drain. Stir in taco sauce. Cook 2 to 3 minutes, stirring occasionally, until heated.

2 In large bowl, toss lettuce, bell pepper, tomatoes, olives and corn chips. Spoon hot beef mixture over lettuce mixture; toss. Sprinkle with cheese. Serve immediately with dressing.

1 Serving: Calories 410 (Calories from Fat 270); Total Fat 30g (Saturated Fat 11g); Cholesterol 85mg; Sodium 710mg; Total Carbohydrate 11g (Dietary Fiber 3g; Sugars 6g); Protein 24g

Asian Pork Salad

Prep Time: 10 min ▮ Start to Finish: 15 min ▮ 4 servings

2 tablespoons reduced-sodium soy sauce
1 tablespoon chili puree with garlic
1 teaspoon sesame oil
$1/2$ lb pork tenderloin, cut into $1^1/_2$x$^1/_2$-inch strips
3 cups coleslaw mix
1 small bell pepper (any color), cut into $^1/_2$-inch strips
1 can (15 oz) black beans, rinsed, drained

1 In tightly-covered container, shake soy sauce, chili puree and oil until well mixed. Remove 1 tablespoon of the soy sauce mixture; reserve remaining mixture. In medium bowl, toss pork with the 1 tablespoon of the soy sauce mixture.

2 Spray 10-inch nonstick skillet with cooking spray; heat over medium-high heat. Cook pork in skillet, stirring occasionally, until no longer pink in center.

3 In large bowl, place pork. Add reserved soy sauce mixture and remaining ingredients; toss until evenly coated.

1 Serving: Calories 220 (Calories from Fat 35); Total Fat 4g (Saturated Fat 1g); Cholesterol 25mg; Sodium 750mg; Total Carbohydrate 28g (Dietary Fiber 10g); Protein 18g

Bacon-Spinach Salad

Prep Time: 15 min ▮ Start to Finish 25 min ▮ 6 servings

4 slices bacon, cut into ¹/₂-inch pieces
3 tablespoons vegetable oil
5 medium green onions, chopped (¹/₃ cup)
2 teaspoons sugar
¹/₂ teaspoon salt
¹/₄ teaspoon pepper
2 tablespoons white or cider vinegar
8 oz washed fresh spinach leaves (9 cups)
2 hard-cooked eggs, sliced

1 In 10-inch skillet, cook bacon over medium heat, stirring occasionally, until crisp. Remove bacon with slotted spoon; drain on paper towels. Drain all but 3 tablespoons bacon fat from skillet (if there aren't 3 tablespoons bacon fat remaining, add enough vegetable oil to bacon fat to equal 3 tablespoons).

2 Add oil, onions, sugar, salt and pepper to bacon fat in skillet. Cook over medium heat 2 to 3 minutes, stirring occasionally, until onions are slightly softened. Stir in vinegar.

3 Place spinach in very large bowl. Pour warm dressing over spinach; toss to coat. Arrange egg slices on top; sprinkle with bacon. Serve immediately.

1 Serving: Calories 135 (Calories from Fat 100); Total Fat 11g (Saturated Fat 2g); Cholesterol 75mg; Sodium 130mg; Total Carbohydrate 4g (Dietary Fiber 1g); Protein 5g

Ten-Minute Ham Salad

Prep Time: 10 min ▍ Start to Finish: 10 min ▍ 6 servings

6 cups bite-size pieces salad greens

2 cups cubed fully cooked smoked ham

$1/3$ cup Italian dressing

2 tablespoons sesame seed, toasted*

1 medium cucumber, thinly sliced

1 medium tomato, cut into thin wedges

2 green onions, thinly sliced (2 tablespoons)

$1/2$ cup shredded Monterey Jack cheese (2 oz)

In a large bowl, place all ingredients except cheese; toss. Add cheese; toss.

*For toasted sesame seeds, cook over medium-low heat 5 to 7 minutes, stirring frequently until browning begins, then stirring constantly until golden brown. Or, bake 8 to 10 minutes, stirring occasionally until golden brown.

1 Serving: Calories 205 (Calories from Fat 125); Total Fat 14g (Saturated Fat 4g); Cholesterol 35mg; Sodium 860mg; Total Carbohydrate 5g (Dietary Fiber 3g); Protein 15g

Italian Ham and Pasta Salad

Prep Time 30 min   Start to Finish: 6 hr 30 min   12 servings

2 packages (10 oz each) frozen chopped broccoli
7 cups uncooked bow-tie (farfalle) pasta (14 oz)
Italian Dressing (see page 150)
2 lb fully cooked ham, cut into julienne strips
1 medium green bell pepper, chopped (1 cup)
1 small onion, finely chopped (¼ cup)

1 Cook broccoli and pasta as directed on packages; drain. Rinse pasta with cold water; drain.

2 Make Italian Dressing. In large bowl, add broccoli, pasta and remaining ingredients to dressing; toss.

3 Cover and refrigerate at least 6 hours or until chilled.

1 Serving: Calories 420 (Calories from Fat 160); Total Fat 18g (Saturated Fat 4g); Cholesterol 45mg; Sodium 1210mg; Total Carbohydrate 41g (Dietary Fiber 3g); Protein 26g

In a hurry? Use 1 cup of your favorite bottled Italian dressing instead of making it from scratch.

Grilled Maple-Dijon Salmon and Asparagus Salad

Summer Salmon Salad

Savory Poached Salmon Salad

Ahi Tuna Salad with Citrus-Cilantro Vinaigrette

Grilled Teriyaki Tuna Salad

Tuna, Tomato and Mozzarella Salad

Italian Tuna Toss

Tuna-Feta Salad

Salad Niçoise

Three-Bean and Tuna Salad

Tuna Salad Sandwiches

Peppered Shrimp and Mango Salad

Caribbean Shrimp Salad

Caesar Shrimp Salad

Spinach-Shrimp Salad with Hot Bacon Dressing

Shrimp Paella Salad

Grilled Shrimp Louis Salad

Seafood-Rice Salad

Snappy Seafood Salad

Chopped Vegetable and Crabmeat Salad

Spicy Coconut Crabmeat Salad

Apple-Fennel Lobster Salad

5

fish and seafood salads

Grilled Maple-Dijon Salmon and Asparagus Salad

Prep Time: 30 min ■ Start to Finish: 30 min ■ 4 servings

Dressing
1/3 cup maple-flavored syrup
2 tablespoons Dijon mustard
2 tablespoons olive or vegetable oil

Salad
1 lb asparagus spears
1 1/2 lb salmon fillets, about 1/2 inch thick, cut into 4 serving pieces
4 cups fresh baby salad greens
1 cup shredded carrots (about 2 medium)
2 hard-cooked eggs, cut into 8 wedges
Freshly ground pepper, if desired

1 Heat gas or charcoal grill. In small bowl, mix all dressing ingredients with whisk.

2 Break off tough ends of asparagus as far down as stalks snap easily. Brush fish with 1 tablespoon of the dressing. In 11 × 7-inch glass baking dish, toss asparagus and 1 tablespoon of the dressing. Place asparagus in grill basket (grill "wok").

3 Place grill basket and fish, skin side down, on grill. Cover grill; cook asparagus over medium heat 7 to 10 minutes, shaking grill basket or turning asparagus occasionally, until crisp-tender. Cook fish 10 to 15 minutes or until fish flakes easily with fork.

4 Slide pancake turner between fish and skin to remove each piece from skin. Among 4 plates, divide salad greens, carrots and eggs. Top with fish and asparagus. Sprinkle with pepper. Serve with remaining dressing.

1 Serving: Calories 420 (Calories from Fat 170); Total Fat 19g (Saturated Fat 4g); Cholesterol 200mg; Sodium 370mg; Total Carbohydrate 27g (Dietary Fiber 3g); Protein 37g

Summer Salmon Salad

Prep Time: 30 min ▪ Start to Finish: 30 min ▪ 4 servings

Toasted Sesame Dressing
1 tablespoon sesame seed, toasted*
1/8 cup white wine vinegar
1 tablespoon sugar
2 tablespoons olive or vegetable oil
1 teaspoon ground mustard
1/2 teaspoon salt
1 large clove garlic, finely chopped

Salad
1 small zucchini, thinly sliced
1 small yellow summer squash,
   thinly sliced (1 1/2 cups)
4 roma (plum) tomatoes, thinly sliced
1 small onion, sliced and separated
   into rings
1 cup sliced mushrooms (3 oz)
Lettuce leaves
1 can (14 3/4 oz) salmon, chilled,
   drained and flaked

1 In tightly-covered container, shake dressing ingredients until well mixed.

2 In large bowl, toss zucchini, summer squash, tomatoes, onion and mushrooms.

3 Line 4 salad plates with lettuce leaves. Spoon vegetable mixture onto lettuce leaves. Place salmon on center of vegetable mixture. Spoon dressing over salads.

*To toast sesame seeds, bake uncovered in ungreased shallow pan in 350°F oven 8 to 10 minutes, stirring occasionally, until golden brown. Or cook in ungreased heavy skillet over medium-low heat 5 to 7 minutes, stirring frequently until browning begins, then stirring constantly until golden brown.

1 Serving: Calories 270 (Calories from Fat 135); Total Fat 15g (Saturated Fat 3g); Cholesterol 60mg; Sodium 880mg; Total Carbohydrate 11g (Dietary Fiber 2g); Protein 23g

If you have sesame seed oil in your pantry, use it in place of the olive oil and omit the sesame seed.

Savory Poached Salmon Salad

Prep Time: 20 min ▪ Start to Finish: 20 min ▪ 6 servings

Salad

1 lb salmon or other medium-firm fish steaks (1 inch thick)

¼ teaspoon salt

¼ cup dry white wine or chicken broth

6 cups shredded lettuce

½ cup croutons

¼ cup chopped fresh parsley

½ small red onion, sliced, separated into rings

Dijon Vinaigrette

¼ cup vegetable oil

2 tablespoons finely chopped green onions (2 medium)

2 tablespoons lemon juice

2 teaspoons chopped fresh or ½ teaspoon dried tarragon leaves

1 teaspoon Dijon mustard

Dash freshly ground pepper

1 In 8-inch square microwavable dish, arrange fish, thickest parts to outside edges. Sprinkle with salt. Pour wine over fish. Cover with plastic wrap, folding back one edge or corner to vent steam. Microwave on High 6 to 8 minutes or until fish flakes easily with fork. Let stand covered 3 minutes; drain. Remove skin and bones; break salmon into 1-inch pieces.

2 In large bowl, gently toss salmon with lettuce, croutons, parsley and onion.

3 In tightly-covered container, shake vinaigrette ingredients until well mixed. Drizzle over salad; gently toss until evenly coated.

1 Serving: Calories 210 (Calories from Fat 120); Total Fat 13g (Saturated Fat 2.5g); Cholesterol 40mg; Sodium 180mg; Total Carbohydrate 5g (Dietary Fiber 1g); Protein 14g

Ahi Tuna Salad with Citrus-Cilantro Vinaigrette

Prep Time: 30 min ▪ Start to Finish: 30 min ▪ 4 servings

Vinaigrette

1 teaspoon grated orange peel
1/2 cup fresh orange juice
1 tablespoon chopped fresh cilantro
1 tablespoon lemon juice
1 tablespoon Dijon mustard
1 tablespoon honey
1/8 teaspoon salt
1/8 teaspoon pepper

Salad

4 sashimi-grade ahi tuna fillets
   (4 oz each)
1 teaspoon olive oil
1/2 teaspoon salt
1/2 teaspoon pepper
6 cups loosely packed mixed salad
   greens
24 small mandarin orange segments
2 tablespoons chopped green onions
   (2 medium)
2 teaspoons sliced almonds

1 In small bowl, beat all vinaigrette ingredients with whisk until well blended. Cover; refrigerate.

2 Lightly brush both sides of tuna fillets with oil; sprinkle with 1/2 teaspoon each salt and pepper. In 12-inch nonstick skillet, cook tuna over medium-high heat 1 minute on each side for rare doneness. Place on plate; refrigerate 5 to 10 minutes.

3 On cutting board, cut tuna into 1/4-inch slices.

4 On each of 4 plates, arrange 1 1/2 cups greens; top with 6 orange segments, 1 1/2 teaspoons onions and 1/2 teaspoon almonds. Arrange tuna on greens. Drizzle 3 tablespoons dressing over tuna and greens on each plate.

1 Serving: Calories 220 (Calories from Fat 70); Total Fat 8g (Saturated Fat 2g); Cholesterol 65mg; Sodium 550mg; Total Carbohydrate 14g (Dietary Fiber 3g); Protein 24g

Grilled Teriyaki Tuna Salad

Prep Time: 25 min ■ Start to Finish: 25 min ■ 4 servings

Dressing
1/2 cup pineapple juice
1/4 cup teriyaki baste and glaze (from 12-oz bottle)
1 tablespoon sesame oil
1/4 teaspoon ground ginger

Salad
12 pieces (1 1/2 inches each) fresh pineapple (2 cups)
1 1/2 lb tuna steaks, about 3/4 inch thick, cut into 4 serving pieces
4 cups bite-size pieces mixed salad greens
1 cup grape or cherry tomatoes, cut in half
1 small red onion, sliced and separated into rings
1/2 cup sesame oat bran sticks or croutons

1 Spray grill rack with cooking spray. Heat gas or charcoal grill. In small bowl, mix all dressing ingredients with whisk; reserve 2 tablespoons.

2 On each of 2 (10-inch) metal skewers, thread pineapple, leaving 1/4-inch space between each piece. Brush 1 tablespoon of the reserved dressing on pineapple; brush remaining 1 tablespoon reserved dressing on fish.

3 Place fish on grill. Cover grill; cook over medium heat about 10 minutes, turning once and adding pineapple for last 5 minutes of grilling, until fish flakes easily with fork.

4 Among 4 plates, divide salad greens, tomatoes and onion. Top with pineapple and tuna. Sprinkle with sesame sticks. Serve with remaining dressing.

1 Serving: Calories 420 (Calories from Fat 140); Total Fat 15g (Saturated Fat 3.5g); Cholesterol 100mg; Sodium 710mg; Total Carbohydrate 35g (Dietary Fiber 4g); Protein 36g

Keeping a few bastes in your pantry lets you grill at a moment's notice. One of the most versatile is teriyaki baste and glaze. It has a thick, syrup-like consistency and shouldn't be confused with teriyaki marinade or sauce, which is more watery.

Tuna, Tomato and Mozzarella Salad

Prep Time: 20 min ■ Start to Finish: 30 min ■ 3 servings

1/2 lb tuna or other firm fish steaks

1 teaspoon olive or vegetable oil

1 small clove garlic, finely chopped

3 large plum (Roma) tomatoes, sliced lengthwise

4 oz fresh mozzarella cheese, sliced

2 tablespoons balsamic vinaigrette

2 tablespoons chopped fresh basil leaves

1 Heat gas or charcoal grill. Drizzle both sides of tuna steaks with oil; rub with garlic. Let stand at room temperature 15 minutes to marinate.

2 Meanwhile, arrange tomato and cheese slices on large serving plate or platter. Drizzle with vinaigrette; sprinkle with basil. Set aside.

3 Cover and grill tuna 4 to 6 inches from medium heat 8 to 10 minutes or until fish flakes easily with fork, turning once. Cut tuna into slices; place on top of tomatoes and cheese.

1 Serving: Calories 290 (Calories from Fat 160); Total Fat 18g (Saturated Fat 7g); Cholesterol 65mg; Sodium 320mg; Total Carbohydrate 7g (Dietary Fiber 1g); Protein 25g

Italian Tuna Toss

Prep Time: 15 min ▪ Start to Finish: 15 min ▪ 6 to 8 servings

1 bag (10 oz) salad mix (about 8 cups)
1 bag (16 oz) fresh cauliflorets
1 medium cucumber, sliced (1½ cups)
2 cans (6 oz each) tuna in water, drained
1 jar (2 oz) sliced pimientos, drained (¼ cup)
⅓ cup Italian dressing
¼ cup bacon-flavor bits or chips

In large bowl, toss all ingredients except dressing and bacon bits. Add dressing and bacon bits; toss.

1 Serving: Calories 175 (Calories from Fat 65); Total Fat 7g (Saturated Fat 1g); Cholesterol 20mg; Sodium 400mg; Total Carbohydrate 9g (Dietary Fiber 4g); Protein 19g

You can also separate a small head of cauliflower into florets instead of using the bag of florets. One small head will yield about 3 cups. Instead of the bag of greens, you can use a small bunch of curly endive or romaine, torn into bite-size pieces.

Tuna-Feta Salad

Prep Time: 10 min ▪ Start to Finish: 1 hr 10 min ▪ 8 servings

Salad
2 cans (15 to 16 oz each) cannellini or other white beans, rinsed, drained
1 can (9 oz) chunk light tuna in water, drained, flaked
1/3 cup crumbled feta cheese
1 medium Spanish, Bermuda or red onion, thinly sliced
Chopped fresh parsley

Red Wine Vinaigrette
1/3 cup olive or vegetable oil
3 tablespoons red wine vinegar
1/2 teaspoon salt
Freshly ground pepper

1 In shallow glass or plastic dish, mix beans, tuna, cheese and onion. In tightly-covered container, shake vinaigrette ingredients until well mixed; pour over bean mixture. Cover and refrigerate at least 1 hour or overnight, stirring occasionally.

2 Transfer bean mixture to serving platter with slotted spoon. Sprinkle with parsley.

1 Serving: Calories 250 (Calories from Fat 100); Total Fat 11g (Saturated Fat 2.5g); Cholesterol 10mg; Sodium 550mg; Total Carbohydrate 23g (Dietary Fiber 5g); Protein 14g

Salad Niçoise

Prep Time: 20 min ▪ Start to Finish: 1 hr 20 min ▪ 4 servings

2 cups frozen French-style green beans (from 1-lb bag)
³/₄ cup Classic French Dressing (page 150)
1 head Bibb lettuce, torn into bite-size pieces (4 cups)
2 medium tomatoes, cut into sixths
2 hard-cooked eggs, cut into fourths
1 can (6 oz) tuna in water, drained, flaked
2 tablespoons sliced ripe olives
Chopped fresh parsley, if desired
6 anchovy fillets, if desired

1 Cook and drain green beans as directed on bag. Refrigerate at least 1 hour until chilled.

2 Make Classic French Dressing.

3 Place lettuce in deep platter or salad bowl. Arrange green beans, tomatoes and eggs around edge of lettuce. Mound tuna in center; sprinkle with olives. Sprinkle parsley over salad. Garnish with anchovies. Serve with dressing. Serve immediately, or cover and refrigerate until serving time.

1 Serving: Calories 345 (Calories from Fat 225); Total Fat 26g (Saturated Fat 4g); Cholesterol 120mg; Sodium 310mg; Total Carbohydrate 12g (Dietary Fiber 4g); Protein 16g

Three-Bean and Tuna Salad

Prep Time: 20 min ■ Start to Finish: 20 min ■ 4 servings

Lemon Vinaigrette
1/4 cup olive or vegetable oil
2 tablespoons lemon juice
1/4 teaspoon red pepper sauce

Salad
1 can (15 to 16 oz) cannellini beans, rinsed, drained
1 can (15 to 16 oz) kidney beans, rinsed, drained
1 can (15 to 16 oz) cut green beans, rinsed, drained
1 large bell pepper, chopped (1 1/2 cups)
1 medium onion, chopped (1/2 cup)
1/4 cup chopped fresh parsley
Lettuce leaves
1 can (6 oz) tuna in water, drained
Lemon wedges, if desired

1 In tightly-covered container, shake all vinaigrette ingredients.

2 In large bowl, mix beans, bell pepper, onion and parsley. Pour vinaigrette over bean mixture; toss.

3 Line 4 salad plates with lettuce leaves. Spoon bean mixture over lettuce. Top with tuna. Serve with lemon wedges.

1 Serving: Calories 365 (Calories from Fat 135); Total Fat 15g (Saturated Fat 3g); Cholesterol 10mg; Sodium 790mg; Total Carbohydrate 45g (Dietary Fiber 12g); Protein 25g

For a super shortcut, use 1/3 cup Italian dressing in place of the Lemon Vinaigrette.

Tuna Salad Sandwiches

Prep Time: 15 min ▪ Start to Finish: 15 min ▪ 4 sandwiches

2 cans (6 oz each) tuna in water, drained
1 medium stalk celery, chopped (1/2 cup)
1 small onion, chopped (1/4 cup)
1/2 cup mayonnaise or salad dressing
1 teaspoon lemon juice
1/4 teaspoon salt
1/4 teaspoon pepper
8 slices bread

1 In medium bowl, mix all ingredients except bread.

2 Spread tuna mixture on 4 bread slices. Top with remaining bread slices.

1 Sandwich: Calories 410 (Calories from Fat 210); Total Fat 24g (Saturated Fat 4g); Cholesterol 30mg; Sodium 870mg; Total Carbohydrate 29g (Dietary Fiber 1g); Protein 21g

Lighter Tuna Salad Sandwiches: Use fat-free mayonnaise for a tuna salad sandwich with 3 grams of fat and 240 calories.

Chicken Salad Sandwiches: Substitute 1½ cups chopped cooked chicken or turkey for the tuna. Omit the lemon juice.

Egg Salad Sandwiches: Substitute 6 hard-cooked eggs, chopped, for the tuna. Omit the lemon juice.

Ham Salad Sandwiches: Substitute 1½ cups chopped cooked ham for the tuna. Omit the salt and pepper. Substitute 1 teaspoon yellow mustard for the lemon juice.

Peppered Shrimp
and Mango Salad

Prep Time: 15 min ▪ Start to Finish: 15 min ▪ 4 servings

20 uncooked deveined peeled large shrimp, thawed
    if frozen, tail shells removed (about $3/4$ lb)
$1/2$ teaspoon salt
$1/2$ teaspoon pepper
1 tablespoon sesame or vegetable oil
1 bag (5 oz) ready-to-eat mixed salad greens
$1 1/2$ cups diced mangoes (about $1 1/2$ medium)
$1/2$ cup sliced radishes (about 5 medium)
$1/3$ cup Asian sesame dressing

1 In medium bowl, toss shrimp with salt and pepper.

2 In 10-inch skillet, heat oil over high heat. Add shrimp; cook about 3 minutes, stirring frequently, until shrimp are pink. Remove from heat.

3 In large bowl, toss salad greens, mangoes, radishes and dressing. Top with shrimp.

1 Serving: Calories 200 (Calories from Fat 120); Total Fat 13g (Saturated Fat 2g); Cholesterol 60mg; Sodium 590mg; Total Carbohydrate 13g (Dietary Fiber 2g); Protein 7g

Caribbean Shrimp Salad

Prep Time: 20 min ▪ Start to Finish: 20 min ▪ 4 servings

Honey-Lime Dressing

3 tablespoons honey

1 teaspoon grated lime peel

2 tablespoons lime juice

1 tablespoon vegetable oil

1 to 2 teaspoons finely chopped jalapeño chili

1/4 teaspoon salt

Salad

1 bag (5 oz) mixed spring greens

1 lb cooked deveined peeled medium shrimp,
   thawed if frozen, tails removed

1 small red onion, thinly sliced

1 can (15 1/4 oz) pineapple shapes, drained

1 cup snow pea pods, strings removed

1 In small bowl, mix all dressing ingredients.

2 In large bowl, mix all salad ingredients. Add dressing; toss until coated.

1 Serving: Calories 285 (Calories from Fat 45); Total Fat 5g (Saturated Fat 1g); Cholesterol 220mg; Sodium 410mg; Total Carbohydrate 34g (Dietary Fiber 2g); Protein 26g

Caesar Shrimp Salad

Prep Time: 25 min ■ Start to Finish: 25 min ■ 8 servings

4 cups uncooked medium pasta shells (10 oz)

1 cup shredded Parmesan cheese (4 oz)

1 cup reduced-fat creamy Caesar dressing

8 medium green onions, sliced (1/2 cup)

1 1/2 lb frozen cooked deveined peeled shrimp, thawed, drained and tail shells
    removed

1 bag (10 oz) ready-to-eat romaine lettuce (7 cups)

2 cups Caesar-flavored croutons

1 Cook and drain pasta as directed on package. Rinse with cold water; drain.

2 In very large (4-quart) bowl, place pasta, cheese, dressing, onions and shrimp; toss. Just before serving, add lettuce and croutons; toss.

1 Serving: Calories 370 (Calories from Fat 80); Total Fat 9g (Saturated Fat 3.5g); Cholesterol 180mg; Sodium 1000mg; Total Carbohydrate 42g (Dietary Fiber 4g); Protein 30g

Crisp breadsticks are perfect with this salad. The cracker aisle usually has plain and flavored versions that are either long and skinny or shorter and a bit wider.

Spinach-Shrimp Salad with Hot Bacon Dressing

Prep Time: 10 min ▪ Start to Finish: 20 min ▪ 4 servings

4 slices bacon, cut into 1-inch pieces

$\frac{1}{4}$ cup white vinegar

1 tablespoon sugar

$\frac{1}{4}$ teaspoon ground mustard

4 cups lightly packed bite-size pieces spinach leaves

1 cup sliced mushrooms (3 oz)

1 cup crumbled feta cheese (4 oz)

$\frac{1}{2}$ lb cooked deveined peeled medium shrimp,
    thawed if frozen, tail shells removed

1 In 10-inch skillet, cook bacon over medium-high heat, stirring occasionally, until crisp. Stir in vinegar, sugar and mustard; continue stirring until sugar is dissolved.

2 In large bowl, toss spinach, mushrooms, cheese and shrimp. Drizzle hot bacon dressing over spinach mixture; toss. Serve immediately.

1 Serving: Calories 210 (Calories from Fat 100); Total Fat 11g (Saturated Fat 6g); Cholesterol 140mg; Sodium 570mg; Total Carbohydrate 7g (Dietary Fiber 1g); Protein 20g

Instead of plain feta, try using crumbled feta flavored with sun-dried tomatoes or basil-and-tomato in this easy-to-fix salad recipe.

Shrimp Paella Salad

Prep Time: 20 min ▪ Start to Finish: 20 min ▪ 2 servings

2 slices bacon, cut up
1 clove garlic, finely chopped
1 cup cooked rice
$1/2$ cup frozen sweet peas, thawed
2 tablespoons chopped drained roasted red bell
    peppers (from 7-oz jar)
1 tablespoon lemon juice
$1/8$ teaspoon paprika
2 or 3 drops red pepper sauce
6 oz cooked peeled deveined medium shrimp,
    thawed if frozen, tail shells removed
Lettuce leaves

1 In 10-inch skillet, cook bacon until crisp. Drain bacon on paper towel, reserving 1 tablespoon drippings in skillet.

2 Cook and stir garlic in bacon drippings over medium heat until softened, about 1 minute. Stir in bacon and remaining ingredients except lettuce.

3 On 2 plates, place lettuce. Top with shrimp mixture; sprinkle with additional paprika.

1 Serving: Calories 250 (Calories from Fat 45); Total Fat 5g (Saturated Fat 1.5g); Cholesterol 175mg; Sodium 650mg; Total Carbohydrate 29g (Dietary Fiber 2g); Protein 24g

Instead of serving the salad on a bed of lettuce, turn it into lettuce wraps. Fill Bibb or iceberg lettuce leaves with the shrimp mixture, roll and enjoy. Double this recipe for guests and let everyone fill their own.

Grilled Shrimp Louis Salad

Prep Time: 25 min ▪ Start to Finish: 25 min ▪ 2 servings

Salad

$1/2$ lb uncooked deveined peeled medium (31 to 35 count) shrimp,
   thawed if frozen, tail shells removed

1 teaspoon olive or canola oil

$1/8$ teaspoon salt

4 cups chopped romaine lettuce

$1/2$ cup finely chopped celery (1 medium stalk)

$1/2$ cup chopped red bell pepper

1 cup grape tomatoes, cut in half

Dressing

2 tablespoons reduced-fat mayonnaise or salad dressing

1 tablespoon plain low-fat yogurt

1 tablespoon shrimp cocktail sauce

$1/2$ teaspoon grated lemon peel

$1/8$ teaspoon salt

1 to 2 tablespoons fat-free (skim) milk

1 Heat gas or charcoal grill. On each of 2 (12-inch) metal skewers, thread shrimp, leaving ¼-inch space between each shrimp. Brush with oil. Sprinkle with ⅛ teaspoon salt.

2 Place kabobs on grill over medium heat. Cover grill; cook 4 to 6 minutes, turning once, until shrimp are pink.

3 On 2 serving plates, arrange lettuce. Top with celery, bell pepper and tomatoes. Remove shrimp from skewers; place on tomatoes.

4 In small bowl, mix all dressing ingredients, adding enough milk for desired consistency. Spoon dressing onto centers of salads.

1 Serving: Calories 220 (Calories from Fat 80); Total Fat 9g (Saturated Fat 1.5g); Cholesterol 165mg; Sodium 720mg; Total Carbohydrate 14g (Dietary Fiber 4g); Protein 21g

Seafood-Rice Salad

Prep Time: 25 min ▪ Start to Finish: 25 min ▪ 10 servings

Lemon Vinaigrette

¹/₂ cup vegetable oil

¹/₂ cup lemon juice

2 tablespoons chopped fresh chives

1 tablespoon grated lemon peel

1 teaspoon Dijon mustard

1 teaspoon sugar

Salad

2 lb cooked scallops

1 lb cooked medium shrimp (31 to 35 count), deveined peeled,
    thawed if frozen, tail shells removed

4 cups cooked rice

3 cups broccoli florets, cooked (8 oz)

2 packages (6 oz each) frozen ready-to-serve crabmeat, thawed, drained

1 In small bowl, mix all vinaigrette ingredients.

2 In large bowl, mix all ingredients except vinaigrette. Toss salad with vinaigrette.

1 Serving: Calories 295 (Calories from Fat 115); Total Fat 13g (Saturated Fat 2g); Cholesterol 90mg; Sodium 270mg; Total Carbohydrate 22g (Dietary Fiber 1g); Protein 24g

Looking for a shortcut? If your supermarket offers a salad bar, you'll find freshly steamed broccoli florets waiting for you there. Just purchase the amount you need and toss this fresh, lemony salad together in no time.

Snappy Seafood Salad

Prep Time: 15 min ■ Start to Finish: 15 min ■ 4 servings

2 cups uncooked medium pasta shells (5 oz)

$^2/_3$ cup mayonnaise or salad dressing

1 tablespoon chili sauce or cocktail sauce

$^1/_3$ cup small pitted ripe olives

3 cups bite-size pieces lettuce

1 package (8 oz) frozen imitation crabmeat, thawed

1 small tomato, cut into 8 wedges

1 Cook and drain pasta as directed on package. Rinse with cold water; drain.

2 In large bowl, mix mayonnaise and chili sauce. Add pasta and olives; toss. Add lettuce and seafood; toss. Serve with tomato wedges.

1 Serving: Calories 480 (Calories from Fat 290); Total Fat 32g (Saturated Fat 5g); Cholesterol 40mg; Sodium 870mg; Total Carbohydrate 36g (Dietary Fiber 2g); Protein 14g

It's a snap to put this summer seafood salad together. Dress it up and add a nice texture and flavor with tender, young salad greens that you can purchase premixed in place of the lettuce.

Chopped Vegetable and Crabmeat Salad

Prep Time: 20 min ▪ Start to Finish: 20 min ▪ 4 servings

Lime Dressing

$1/3$ cup frozen (thawed) limeade concentrate

$1/4$ cup vegetable oil

1 tablespoon rice or white vinegar

1 teaspoon grated gingerroot

$1/4$ teaspoon salt

Salad

2 cups chopped escarole

2 cans (6 oz each) crabmeat, drained and flaked, or 2 cups
    chopped cooked turkey or chicken

1 small jicama, peeled, chopped (1 cup)

1 large papaya, peeled, seeded and chopped (1 cup)

1 medium yellow or red bell pepper, chopped (1 cup)

$1/2$ cup dry-roasted peanuts

$1/4$ cup chopped fresh cilantro

1 In tightly-covered container, shake all dressing ingredients.

2 In large bowl, place ingredients except peanuts and cilantro. Pour dressing over salad; toss. Top with peanuts and cilantro.

1 Serving: Calories 430 (Calories from Fat 215); Total Fat 24g (Saturated Fat 4g); Cholesterol 75mg; Sodium 590mg; Total Carbohydrate 37g (Dietary Fiber 9g); Protein 25g

To get a head start on dinner, chop the papaya and bell pepper, wrap separately and refrigerate. You can also make the dressing a day ahead and refrigerate it.

Spicy Coconut Crabmeat Salad

Prep Time: 15 min ▮ Start to Finish: 15 min ▮ 6 servings

Curry Dressing

1 cup light mayonnaise or salad dressing

1 to 2 teaspoons red curry paste (from 4-oz jar)

1 tablespoon fresh lemon juice

Salad

2 packages (8 oz each) refrigerated chunk-style imitation crabmeat

2 cups fresh sugar snap peas, trimmed, cut in half diagonally

1 cup shredded coconut

½ cup sliced green onions (about 8 medium)

6 cups thinly sliced Chinese (napa) cabbage

1 In large bowl, beat dressing ingredients with whisk until blended.

2 Add imitation crabmeat, peas, coconut and onions; gently toss until evenly coated with dressing. On 6 plates, arrange cabbage. Top with salad mixture.

1 Serving: Calories 250 (Calories from Fat 90); Total Fat 10g (Saturated Fat 6g); Cholesterol 35mg; Sodium 1130mg; Total Carbohydrate 25g (Dietary Fiber 3g); Protein 14g

Apple-Fennel Lobster Salad

Prep Time: 15 min ▪ Start to Finish: 15 min ▪ 4 servings

2 packages (6 oz each) refrigerated salad-style imitation lobster
1 red apple, halved, cored and thinly sliced (1 cup)
1 fennel bulb, cut in half, thinly sliced (1¼ cups)
¼ cup golden raisins
⅓ cup mayonnaise or salad dressing
½ teaspoon salt
½ teaspoon ground mustard
2 tablespoons frozen apple juice concentrate, thawed, or apple juice
4 cups torn romaine lettuce
½ cup chopped walnuts, if desired

1 In medium bowl, mix imitation lobster, apple, fennel and raisins.

2 In small bowl, beat mayonnaise, salt, mustard and apple juice concentrate with whisk until well blended. Pour over lobster mixture; toss.

3 Among 4 plates, divide lettuce. Top with lobster salad. Sprinkle with walnuts.

1 Serving: Calories 300 (Calories from Fat 140); Total Fat 16g (Saturated Fat 2.5g); Cholesterol 30mg; Sodium 1160mg; Total Carbohydrate 25g (Dietary Fiber 3g); Protein 15g

Like them tart or sweet, crisp or soft? It doesn't matter; just use your favorite apple in this upscale, bistro-style salad. Reserve the frilly fronds of the fennel bulb for a very pretty garnish.

Italian Dressing

Classic French Dressing

Thousand Island Dressing

Honey-Dijon Dressing

Fresh Herb Vinaigrette

Raspberry Vinaigrette

Asian Dressing

Buttermilk Ranch Dressing

Blue Cheese Dressing

6
salad dressings

Italian Dressing

Prep Time: 10 min ▪ Start to Finish: 10 min ▪ About 1¼ cups dressing

1 cup olive or vegetable oil
¼ cup white or cider vinegar
2 tablespoons finely chopped onion
1 tablespoon chopped fresh or
   1 teaspoon dried basil leaves
1 teaspoon sugar

1 teaspoon ground mustard
½ teaspoon salt
½ teaspoon dried oregano leaves
¼ teaspoon pepper
2 cloves garlic, finely chopped

In tightly-covered container, shake all ingredients. Shake before serving. Store tightly covered in refrigerator.

1 Serving (1 tablespoon): Calories 105 (Calories from Fat 100); Total Fat 11g (Saturated Fat 1g); Cholesterol 0mg; Sodium 60mg; Total Carbohydrate 1g (Dietary Fiber 0g); Protein 0g

Lighter Italian Dressing: For 5 grams of fat and 50 calories per serving, substitute ½ cup apple juice for ½ cup of the oil.

Classic French Dressing

Prep Time: 5 min ▪ Start to Finish: 5 min ▪ About 1½ cups dressing

1 cup olive or vegetable oil
¼ cup white or cider vinegar
¼ cup lemon juice
½ teaspoon salt
½ teaspoon ground mustard
½ teaspoon paprika

In tightly-covered container, shake all ingredients. Shake before serving. Store tightly covered in refrigerator.

1 Serving (1 tablespoon): Calories 80 (Calories from Fat 80); Total Fat 9g (Saturated Fat 1g); Cholesterol 0mg; Sodium 50mg; Total Carbohydrates 0g (Dietary Fiber 0g); Protein 0g

Classic Red French Dressing: Mix ½ cup Classic French Dressing and ½ cup ketchup.

Thousand Island Dressing

Prep Time: 15 min ▮ Start to Finish: 15 min ▮ About 1 cup dressing

1 cup mayonnaise or salad dressing
1 tablespoon chopped fresh parsley
2 tablespoons chopped pimiento-
 stuffed olives or sweet pickle
 relish

2 tablespoons chili sauce or
 ketchup
1 teaspoon finely chopped onion
$1/2$ teaspoon paprika
1 hard-cooked egg, finely chopped

In small bowl, mix all ingredients. Store tightly covered in refrigerator.

1 Serving (1 tablespoon): Calories 105 (Calories from Fat 100); Total Fat 11g (Saturated Fat 2g); Cholesterol 20mg; Sodium 135mg; Total Carbohydrates 1g (Dietary Fiber 0g); Protein 1g

Lighter Thousand Island Dressing: For 5 grams of
fat and 55 calories per serving, use reduced-fat mayonnaise; substitute 2 hard-cooked egg whites for the hard-cooked whole egg.

Russian Dressing: Omit parsley, olives and egg. Increase chili
sauce to $1/4$ cup. Add 1 teaspoon prepared horseradish

Honey-Dijon Dressing

Prep Time: 5 min ▮ Start to Finish: 5 min ▮ About 1 cup dressing

$1/2$ cup vegetable oil
$1/3$ cup honey
$1/4$ cup lemon juice
1 tablespoon Dijon mustard

In tightly-covered container, shake all ingredients. Shake before serving. Store tightly covered in refrigerator.

1 Serving (1 tablespoon): Calories 85 (Calories from Fat 65); Total Fat 7g (Saturated Fat 1g); Cholesterol 0mg; Sodium 15mg; Total Carbohydrate 6g (Dietary Fiber 0g); Protein 0g

Honey–Poppy Seed Dressing: Omit mustard. Add
1 tablespoon poppy seed.

Fresh Herb Vinaigrette

Prep Time: 10 min ▯ Start to Finish: 10 min ▯ About ³/₄ cup vinaigrette

¹/₂ cup olive or vegetable oil

3 tablespoons red or white wine vinegar

1 tablespoon chopped fresh herb leaves (such as basil, marjoram, oregano, rosemary, tarragon or thyme)

1 tablespoon chopped fresh parsley

1 medium green onion, finely chopped (1 tablespoon)

³/₄ teaspoon salt

¹/₄ teaspoon pepper

In tightly-covered container, shake all ingredients. Shake before serving. Store tightly covered in refrigerator.

1 Serving (1 tablespoon): Calories 80 (Calories from Fat 80); Total Fat 9g (Saturated Fat 1g); Cholesterol 0mg; Sodium 55mg; Total Carbohydrate 0g (Dietary Fiber 0g); Protein 0g

Raspberry Vinaigrette

Prep Time: 10 min ▯ Start to Finish: 10 min ▯ 1 cup vinaigrette

¹/₃ cup seedless raspberry jam

¹/₂ cup red wine vinegar

¹/₄ cup olive or vegetable oil

¹/₄ teaspoon salt

In small glass or plastic bowl, beat all ingredients with whisk until well blended. Store tightly covered in refrigerator.

1 Serving (1 tablespoon): Calories 45 (Calories from Fat 25); Total Fat 3g (Saturated Fat 0g); Cholesterol 0mg; Sodium 40mg; Total Carbohydrate 5g (Dietary Fiber 0g); Protein 0g

Asian Dressing

Prep Time: 5 min ▪ Start to Finish: 5 min ▪ About 1 cup dressing

$1/3$ cup rice, white or cider vinegar

$1/4$ cup vegetable oil

3 tablespoons soy sauce

1 tablespoon sesame seed, toasted if desired (see page 122)

2 tablespoons dry sherry or apple juice

1 teaspoon grated gingerroot or $1/4$ teaspoon ground ginger

2 drops dark sesame oil, if desired

In tightly-covered container, shake all ingredients. Shake before serving. Store tightly covered in refrigerator.

1 Serving (1 tablespoon): Calories 30 (Calories from Fat 25); Total Fat 3g (Saturated Fat 0g); Cholesterol 0mg; Sodium 170mg; Total Carbohydrate 1g (Dietary Fiber 0g); Protein 0g

Buttermilk Ranch Dressing

Prep Time: 5 min ▪ Start to Finish: 2 hr 5 min ▪ About $1^{1}/4$ cups dressing

$3/4$ cup mayonnaise or salad dressing

$1/2$ cup buttermilk

1 teaspoon parsley flakes

$1/2$ teaspoon instant minced onion

$1/2$ teaspoon salt

Dash of freshly ground pepper

1 clove garlic, finely chopped

In small bowl, mix all ingredients. Cover and refrigerate at least 2 hours to blend flavors. Store tightly covered in refrigerator.

1 Serving (1 tablespoon): Calories 70 (Calories from Fat 70); Total Fat 8g (Saturated Fat 1g); Cholesterol 5mg; Sodium 140mg; Total Carbohydrate 1g (Dietary Fiber 0g); Protein 0g

Lighter Buttermilk Ranch Dressing: For 4 grams of fat and 45 calories per serving, use reduced-fat mayonnaise and buttermilk.

Buttermilk Ranch Parmesan Dressing: Add ⅓ cup grated Parmesan cheese and ½ teaspoon paprika.

Blue Cheese Dressing

Prep Time: 10 min ▪ Start to Finish: 3 hr 10 min ▪ About 1²/₃ cups dressing

³/₄ cup crumbled blue cheese (3 oz)
1 package (3 oz) cream cheese, softened
¹/₂ cup mayonnaise or salad dressing
¹/₃ cup half-and-half

1 Reserve ⅓ cup of the blue cheese. In small bowl, mix remaining blue cheese and the cream cheese until well blended.

2 Stir in mayonnaise and half-and-half until creamy. Stir in reserved ⅓ cup blue cheese. Cover and refrigerate at least 3 hours to blend flavors. Store tightly covered in refrigerator.

1 Serving (1 tablespoon): Calories 60 (Calories from Fat 55); Total Fat 6g (Saturated Fat 2g); Cholesterol 10mg; Sodium 80mg; Total Carbohydrate 0g (Dietary Fiber 0g); Protein 1g

Lighter Blue Cheese Dressing: For 3 grams of fat and 35 calories per serving, decrease blue cheese to ½ cup. Substitute ½ package (8-oz size) reduced-fat cream cheese (Neufchâtel) for the regular cream cheese and ¼ cup fat-free (skim) milk for the half-and-half. Use reduced-fat mayonnaise.

Helpful Nutrition and Cooking Information

Recommended intake for a daily diet of 2,000 calories as set by the Food and Drug Administration

Total Fat	Less than 65g
Saturated Fat	Less than 20g
Cholesterol	Less than 300mg
Sodium	Less than 2,400mg
Total Carbohydrate	300g
Dietary Fiber	25g

Calculating Nutrition Information

The first ingredient was used wherever a choice is given (such as 1/3 cup sour cream or plain yogurt).

The first ingredient amount was used wherever a range is given (such as 3- to 3 1/2-pound cut-up broiler-fryer chicken).

The first serving number was used wherever a range is given (such as 4 to 6 servings).

"If desired" ingredients and recipe variations were not included (such as sprinkle with brown sugar, if desired).

Only the amount of a marinade or frying oil that is estimated to be absorbed by the food during preparation or cooking was calculated.

Ingredients Used in Recipe Testing and Nutrition Calculations

Ingredients used for testing represent those that the majority of consumers use in their homes: large eggs, 2% milk, 80%-lean ground beef, canned ready-to-use chicken broth and vegetable oil spread containing not less than 65% fat.

Fat-free, low-fat or low-sodium products were not used, unless otherwise indicated.

Solid vegetable shortening (not butter, margarine, nonstick cooking sprays or vegetable oil spread as they can cause sticking problems) was used to grease pans, unless otherwise indicated.

Equipment Used in Recipe Testing

We use equipment for testing that the majority of consumers use in their homes. If a specific piece of equipment (such as a whisk) is necessary for recipe success, it is listed in the recipe.

Cookware and bakeware without nonstick coatings were used, unless otherwise indicated.

No dark-colored, black or insulated bakeware was used.

When a pan is specified in a recipe, a metal pan was used; a baking dish or pie plate means ovenproof glass was used.

An electric hand mixer was used for mixing only when mixer speeds are specified in the recipe directions. When a mixer speed is not given, a spoon or fork was used.

Metric Conversion Guide

VOLUME

U.S. Units	Canadian Metric	Australian Metric
¼ teaspoon	1 mL	1 ml
½ teaspoon	2 mL	2 ml
1 teaspoon	5 mL	5 ml
1 tablespoon	15 mL	20 ml
¼ cup	50 mL	60 ml
⅓ cup	75 mL	80 ml
½ cup	125 mL	125 ml
⅔ cup	150 mL	170 ml
¾ cup	175 mL	190 ml
1 cup	250 mL	250 ml
1 quart	1 liter	1 liter
1½ quarts	1.5 liters	1.5 liters
2 quarts	2 liters	2 liters
2½ quarts	2.5 liters	2.5 liters
3 quarts	3 liters	3 liters
4 quarts	4 liters	4 liters

WEIGHT

U.S. Units	Canadian Metric	Australian Metric
1 ounce	30 grams	30 grams
2 ounces	55 grams	60 grams
3 ounces	85 grams	90 grams
4 ounces (¼ pound)	115 grams	125 grams
8 ounces (½ pound)	225 grams	225 grams
16 ounces (1 pound)	455 grams	500 grams
1 pound	455 grams	0.5 kilogram

MEASUREMENTS

Inches	Centimeters
1	2.5
2	5.0
3	7.5
4	10.0
5	12.5
6	15.0
7	17.5
8	20.5
9	23.0
10	25.5
11	28.0
12	30.5
13	33.0

TEMPERATURES

Fahrenheit	Celsius
32°	0°
212°	100°
250°	120°
275°	140°
300°	150°
325°	160°
350°	180°
375°	190°
400°	200°
425°	220°
450°	230°
475°	240°
500°	260°

NOTE: The recipes in this cookbook have not been developed or tested using metric measures. When converting recipes to metric, some variations in quality may be noted.

Index

Page numbers in *italics* refer to photographs.